CODEPENDENCY VS LOVE: BREAKING THE CYCLE

Learn How to Establish Boundaries and Discover Healthy Detachment Principles to Get Away From Toxic, Codependent Relationships, Even if You're in Denial

Table of Contents

Introduction

At first glance, codependent relationships look completely healthy. There appears to be trust, care, and closeness – and what could possibly be bad about that? Look a little closer and you'll see there's more than meets the eye. Both partners appear to have distinct roles and you'll notice they seem to be stuck in a cycle. One partner is the carer or the 'fixer' while the other partner receives an excessive degree of support which holds them back from any personal growth. Now that you see it up close, you recognize this unhealthy pattern for what it is; it's codependency.

If you're in a codependent relationship, you'll know this one-sided dynamic well. Perhaps you're the enabler, intent on helping your partner so much that you end up doing everything for them – even allowing their damaging habits to wreak havoc. Or perhaps you're the enabled partner, suffering from an ailment, addiction, or mental health condition, and you find yourself relying on your significant other a lot to help you get through each day. Until now, you've been taught to believe that your behavior is indicative of love, but I'm here to tell you that you are very wrong.

Codependency is a deeply dysfunctional condition. When it takes over a relationship, it can hold partners back from professional success, sever cords with family members and friends, cause deep emotional or psychological wounding, and in the long run, it'll create resentment in the relationship. This may result in the ruin of the partnership at hand, meaning everything they've lost along the way was all for nothing. As soon as codependency is identified, it must be stopped or this immense damage will be caused.

In this book, I'm going to help you put a stop to your codependent ways so you can finally be in the healthy, happy relationship you desire. I'll take you from clinging codependent partners to empowered individuals who are on top of their respective worlds. Even if you've been stuck in this destructive cycle for a long time, I'll show you how to quit it for good.

I am proud to say I'm a recovered codependent. Since I evolved out of my codependent habits several years ago, I've helped many codependent couples break out of their harmful relationship patterns. I know your struggles better than most people. I've been there and I understand the aching to be needed – and how it feels to not know who you are, when you aren't needed. I'm living proof that it gets better and that your relationship can feel a million times more fulfilling, loving, and empowering, if you just have the right tools and information. That's exactly what I'll be giving you. In this book, I'll be sharing all the insights that I learned on my journey from codependent to completely in power. Everything that I learned the hard way, I'll tell you simply so you don't have to make the same mistakes that I did. I'll show you how I transformed my unhealthy, troubling relationship into a powerful partnership that still thrives to this day – even twenty years down the road!

Your relationship is meant to thrive. Soon, you'll finally understand what that really means. You'll no longer feel desperate and exhausted by your partner. You'll know how to meet your partner's needs while also meeting your own. You'll know how to give your partner the absolute best, while also relishing certain rewards for yourself. For the first time, your relationship will have true balance and you'll experience what it's really like to love deeply, and be deeply loved in return.

I've worked with many couples that others deemed 'too far gone' and they've all seen a full recovery from their codependent ways. Those who once felt stuck, now know what it's like to evolve and grow. The truth is, breaking codependency doesn't just change your relationship, it transforms your entire life. People I've worked with continue to reap the benefits of their self-work to this day. The help I offered them is exactly what I'll be giving you in this book.

Codependent or not, let's not forget that we all want to find ourselves in loving relationships that bring joy to our lives. This is a commonality we all share. What makes you different is you've gotten caught up in the wrong habits and dysfunctional patterns. With my help, you'll finally remove these obstacles. You can enjoy all that is wonderful about your relationship, while leaving behind everything that frustrates and upsets you.

Here's the first tip I'll give you: start now! As time goes on, codependent couples become more fixed in their ways, finding it harder to break their harmful dynamic. Each moment you waste being codependent is a moment you waste not living up to your full potential. What are you and your partner missing out on while you cling to these destructive patterns? What wonderful experiences or accomplishments could be yours *right now* if you just made space for it to bloom?

By turning to the next page, you'll have made the first step to reclaiming your life from codependency. This is an exciting time – the end of a dark era and the rise of a new dawn where you'll finally be free from the shackles of codependency. Get ready for the new chapter of your life.

Chapter 1: Are You Codependent?

Codependency is an uncomfortable topic for many couples and this is partially due to a big misconception about what the term truly means. The word 'codependent' is thrown around a lot in the modern world, used to describe any couple that is extremely close or spends a lot of time together. These definitions are, of course, completely inaccurate. Codependency is many steps above infatuation or intimacy. It is far more than just reliance or dependence. True codependence does a huge disservice to both partners in a relationship, keeping them anchored in unhealthy habits that are slowly ruining their lives. It's about time we stopped using the term 'codependency' so lightly. Its effects can be brutal, if left unchecked.

In a healthy relationship, both partners give and take from each other in equal measure. You do this chore, I'll do that chore. You pay for dinner tonight, I'll cook dinner tomorrow. It may not always be as straightforward as this and there may be times when the exchange is slightly off-balance – for example, during times of stress, illness or trauma – but this in itself is not unhealthy. This in itself is not codependency. It's normal to see this fluctuation over time. Life happens and we're not always at the top of our game. During the low points, dependence on our partner or loved ones is completely natural. So, let's consider an important question: when exactly does reliance cross the line? When does dependence become codependence?

What it Means to Be Codependent

In a codependent relationship, two dysfunctional personalities find the ultimate enabler in each other. One partner desperately needs someone to take care of them and the other partner feels their self-worth is rooted in how much they are needed. These two personalities attract each other like magnets. Without self-awareness or a helpful third party, this can make a pretty toxic cocktail – one that's definitely not sustainable in the long-run. The needed partner takes on the role of 'giver' or 'rescuer' while the needy partner behaves like a troubled victim, 'taking' from the other partner and displaying an excessive need of care. The codependent giver responds to this need for care by overhelping or overextending their assistance.

This is different from everyday reliance in an ordinary relationship because codependency allows unhealthy behavior to continue. While it's completely normal to expect your partner to pick up the groceries sometimes or cook a meal when you're exhausted from work, it's not normal when one partner is consistently acting as the helper. At times, the giver may even take on a parental role, constantly making sure their partner is okay and helping them perform everyday activities they should be able to do themselves. The needy partner gets away with doing very little while the needed partner does nearly everything. Both dysfunctions fuel each other.

The term 'codependency' used to refer strictly to the toxic relationships of addicts and their partners, but today, it has expanded to include any relationship where self-destructive behaviors are allowed to continue. A codependency may enable any of the following behaviors:
- **Addiction** to substances such as drugs, alcohol, gambling, or any other compulsive activities causing financial strain and other damage to their personal life.
- **Poor mental health**, especially destructive symptoms brought about by personality disorders or depression.

9

- **Immaturity** and other forms of irresponsibility, where the enabler feels they have no choice but to accept this behavior because there's no way to change their partner and that's 'just how they are.'
- **Underachievement,** which may or may not be related to any of the above behaviors. The underachieving partner is not pulling their weight financially or giving up on personal goals, and the enabler allows this to continue.

Codependency: So What?

Here's a question I hear a lot: "So what if a couple is codependent? If one partner feels fulfilled as the helper and they happen to find someone that needs to be helped, what's the problem? No one is being forced to do anything they don't want to do! Maybe they're happy this way."

A codependent couple can indeed appear happy, but this brittle happiness rests entirely on their denial. When a codependent partner overhelps their partner, they hold back their loved one from emotional and psychological growth. Destructive behavior is allowed to run rampant. The relationship starts to function like a crutch, where the fragile partner never learns how to take care of their own needs. They no longer feel the urgency to fix their own problems. Instead, they expect someone else to pick up the slack. When a person is treated like a child, they become disempowered and disconnected from their own inner strength. They are not given the opportunity to psychologically mature. This needy attitude affects far more than their romantic life; in fact, it's likely their professional life is suffering too. After all, bosses and coworkers are a lot less understanding than our loving partners!

And matters are just as bad for codependent enablers. They may appear to accomplish more than their partners, but they're also being held back from their full potential. Enablers feel their self-worth is rooted in how needed they are and their ability to help – this is an extremely unhealthy way to determine one's value. Those with this mentality have a hard time recognizing and vocalizing their own needs because they constantly think someone else's needs are more important. Can anyone be truly happy if their needs aren't being met? Many codependent couples stay together for the long-term, but by the end, enablers are often resentful and exhausted by the life they've lived serving someone else, with little care for their own self.

Dependence vs. Codependence

In a loving relationship, it is expected and completely healthy for both partners to depend on each other. This is what being in a relationship is all about! Unfortunately, many codependent couples who fail to see their dysfunctional ways think they're only engaging in healthy dependence. If you're not well-versed in the patterns of codependency, it can be difficult to tell between the two. To help you differentiate between dependence and codependence, let's compare the two types of behavior.

Example #1

Dependent: Partner A is going through a rough time and Partner B feels bad for them. In an attempt to cheer Partner A up, Partner B does something special with hopes it'll make a positive difference. B understands he can't change anything, but he wants to at least bring a smile to A's face.

Codependent: When Partner A starts going through a rough time, Partner B feels he needs to help A solve the problem. Partner B will do everything he can to make his partner feel better. When the attempts

11

don't seem to be working, Partner B will start to feel worthless, like he can't do anything right. Unless he can ease Partner A's suffering, he feels extreme frustration with himself.

Example #2

Dependent: Partner B wants to spend a day in nature alone to destress after an exhausting work week. He tells Partner A his plan and she encourages him to do whatever he needs to do to take care of his mental state. She spends a day enjoying her own hobbies while her partner relaxes by himself. When they reunite at the end of the day, they feel refreshed after some alone time and happy to see each other.

Codependent: Partner B needs to destress alone but he's nervous to ask Partner A in case she takes it the wrong way. When he finally asks Partner A if they can have a day apart, she looks sad but begrudgingly allows him to go. While they're away from each other, they are anxious. Partner B starts to feel guilty for leaving Partner A and he thinks to himself that it was a bad idea. When they reunite at the end of the day, Partner A is sulky and tries to guilt trip Partner B for leaving. Feeling bad, Partner B feels he has to fix it and make it up to her.

Example #3

Dependent: Both partners express what they need to feel valued and taken care of in the relationship. Each person makes their thoughts and feelings known while the other listens closely and thinks of how they can best meet their partner's needs.

Codependent: Partner A expresses her needs while Partner B listens closely and tries to help. Partner A is seen as having more pressing needs since her emotional state is more fragile. Partner B may bring up his concerns, but this gets brushed aside since he believes fragile Partner A has more important needs. Partner A silently agrees that her needs are more important.

It can be exceedingly difficult for people to admit to codependence. The fact of the matter is that codependent partners often have pure intentions at heart; they simply want to help their significant others and ease their suffering. Still, the results are no less counterproductive. In most cases, the dynamic does far more harm than good to both partners involved. If you think you might be in a codependent relationship, it's vital that you recognize this as soon as possible.

Signs You're the Enabler in a Codependent Relationship

The caretaker or 'giver' in a codependent relationship is also called the 'enabler.' This is because, through excessive care, they are enabling their partner's self-destructive behavior. If you tick three or more of the following boxes, then you are most likely the enabler in your relationship.

- You Constantly Give In

When your partner needs or wants something, you always find yourself giving in and doing what they want. Sometimes it will feel unreasonable and you may even resent them for it – but you continue to give in anyway. You end up dismissing your feelings to take care of your partner or keep the peace.

- You Take Responsibility for Their Actions

When a needy partner does something wrong or displays negative behavior, a codependent may find themselves taking responsibility for it. Instead of seeing their partner as the sole person at fault, they will believe they influenced that behavior. Codependent givers constantly make excuses for their partners and they may even blame themselves for it.

- You Perform Simple Tasks They Should Be Doing for Themselves

It's normal to care for our partners, but how often are you required to help with simple tasks that every other adult can accomplish just fine?

Are you the person that gets your partner fed? Do you constantly have to wake them up so they aren't late to appointments? Do you end up finishing the chores that they were supposed to handle?

- You're Always Trying to Fix Everything

You just can't help it. No matter what happens, you're always trying to meet needs that may or may not exist. If your partner isn't feeling his or her best, you feel like it's your responsibility to make them feel better. You may find yourself anticipating their needs and perhaps even trying to fix something that doesn't need to be fixed. In any case, whenever your partner needs anything, you're always there doing everything you can to make it better, even when they're not doing anything to help their own self.

- You Frequently Have to Ask for Your Partner's Approval

For one reason or another, you don't feel like you can do as you please. If you want to make a decision for yourself or have some time away, you feel like you need to check if your partner is okay with this. The reason behind this behavior is likely that you feel your partner may need you and the idea of your partner being alone makes you feel guilty. By getting your partner's approval, this guilt is eliminated.

- You See Your Partner as Helpless

Be honest with yourself here. Imagine your partner being left to their own devices for a whole week. Perhaps you're going away on an important trip to a place with minimal phone reception. Your partner will have to do everything on their own and look after him or herself without any outside help at all. How worried does this thought make you? Do you trust that your partner will be able to take care of him or herself and function properly without you? Will they be able to stay away from their bad habits, eat and sleep well, and get to important appointments on time? If you answered no to any of these questions, admit it to yourself: you believe your partner is helpless.

- When You're Not Taking Care of Your Loved One, You Feel Like a Bad Partner

At the end of the day, you continue giving and enabling because the alternative makes you feel guilty. You worry that if you set any boundaries, this will make matters worse for your partner. You feel that your partner really needs you and the thought of not helping them with everyday activities feels akin to tossing them overboard into the ocean. You are used to providing assistance and when you don't, you feel like you've done something terrible.

Are you in Denial?

One of the major obstacles in codependent relationships is denial. It is a core symptom of codependency. Even with expert advice right in front of you, nothing will help your situation if you can't admit there's something wrong. One of the reasons codependency is allowed to continue is because both partners are in denial about their unhealthy cycle. Before dysfunctions can be treated, it's essential that both partners stop living in denial about their bad habits or the severity of their effects. These are the signs you've been living in denial.

- You dismiss your own feelings and instincts

It's happened before. You've felt something nudge at your mind, saying, "It shouldn't be like this" or "This doesn't feel quite right." Instead of delving deeper into the issue, you always decide to brush this feeling aside. You tell yourself it isn't important or that the feeling is outright silly, even though this isn't the first time you've felt this way. If you often find yourself having to dismiss your instincts, thoughts, or feelings, then there's a good chance you're in denial. If a feeling continues to resurface, chances are that your intuition is correct.

- You're just waiting for change

Perhaps you've admitted to yourself that there needs to be change. What happens after that admission? Do you and your partner take action to remedy the situation immediately? Or do you just sit back and tell yourself it'll change with time? Relying on external influences or other people to change is another red flag you're in denial, especially if you've been 'waiting' for a rather long time. This shows you've given up your power to create change. Instead of making progress yourself, you are waiting for it to fall from the sky. People who do this tend to be in denial about how bad their situation is.

- Everyone sees a problem you don't see

Are there people in your life who insist your relationship is deeply flawed? The more people who have said this to you, the higher the likelihood that they're correct. If you can't see this problem, you're probably in denial about its existence. When we're entrenched in a dysfunctional pattern, sometimes it can be difficult to point it out. People on the outside of your relationship, however, can see the big picture. And the people who are close to you will know you best and what is best for you. If you constantly find yourself defending your relationship to close friends and family, there's a chance you're in denial that what they're saying is true.

Denial protects us from a harsh truth. By pretending not to notice something, we feel there's a possibility we can ignore it out of existence. This could not be further from the truth and in fact, denial can cause more harm than good. If you want to continue healing your relationship, nip your denial in the bud right now. Change only comes when you face reality.

Chapter 2: Understanding Codependent Personalities

What many people fail to realize is that it takes two dependent personalities to create a codependent relationship. These personalities are distinct but equally as problematic as each other. Those on the outside of the relationship have a tendency to blame whichever person is the most needy, but the fact of the matter is it's not just one person's fault. Both personalities carry their own dysfunctional traits, they just manifest in very different ways. When they come together, the worst instincts of these personalities are enabled. One partner's unhealthy behavior is exactly what the other person needs to indulge their own unhealthy behavior. This is how the codependent cycle begins and why it's often difficult to stop.

In order to create a healthier dynamic, it's essential that couples reflect on their individual selves. By now, it should be clear which of the two distinct roles each person in the relationship plays. This identification is step one. When both parties are aware of the role they play in the dynamic, there can finally come a greater understanding of what each person can do to heal the problem. It is important that both personalities are regarded with equal importance. To start making progress, both personalities should be studied and understood. It all starts with you.

Decoding the Enabler

At some point in the enabler's childhood, they were made to believe their needs are always secondary. In early studies of codependency, it was believed that enabling tendencies stemmed from growing up with an alcoholic parent, but today, experts agree there can be many causes.

Alcoholic or not, these issues are usually the result of a needy or otherwise unavailable parent. While it is possible that the enabler was subjected to emotional or physical abuse, this is not always the case. Often, they simply grew up amidst highly dysfunctional family dynamics, and this may or may not involve a physically or mentally ill family member. These codependents did not receive adequate emotional care so they became accustomed to having their needs unmet. Most children grow up receiving a lot of positive validation; in the case of the enabler, they likely did not receive much validation at all. This results in an individual who, by default, does not feel very important. Instead, they've learned to find validation vicariously through someone else.

In the case of a needy or ill family member, the enabler may have had some caretaking responsibilities, thus solidifying their comfort in assuming a caretaking role later on in life. Whatever their childhood story, one thing is absolutely certain: the codependent has been taught their worth and value are directly linked to how much they please others and how well they can take care of other people. This flawed belief is exactly what creates dysfunction in this personality type. In an effort to feel worthy and good about themselves, they will seek out situations where they offer some form of help. The most wounded enablers may even feel that the more lost the cause, the bigger the reward. This can lead them into disastrous relationships, creating severe trauma, and only worsening the dysfunction. Still, many of these deeply wounded enablers continue to try and serve, believing that the problem lies with them and not their partner. It is a vicious cycle that only ends when self-awareness comes.

It's important to note that some enablers act from deep abandonment issues where they feel they must do everything to make their partner happy otherwise they will be abandoned. 'Abandonment' here does not necessarily mean a break-up. If the enabler suffered through the death of a sick parent, they may overhelp their sick partner, fueled by the subconscious fear that they'll have the same experience all over again.

If you're an enabler seeking recovery, it's vital that you figure out where this need to overhelp stems from. At what point in your life were you taught your needs were less important? Who was the person whose needs took priority over your own? Once you've identified this essential detail, you can begin to separate that incident from your current relationship.

Understanding the Enabled Partner

When studying codependent relationships, the enabled individual can be far more difficult to decode. Why? Because, while all enablers possess similar endgames and intentions, their enabled counterparts can have wildly different motives and causes. Many grew up being coddled or spoilt as children, so they started to expect the same treatment from other people close to them. But the flip side is also possible – they may have been neglected as children, causing them to turn to attention-seeking behaviors. If they were coddled as children, it's possible they don't recognize the reality of their situation. They may think it is completely normal to be waited on hand and foot because that's how they've been treated all their lives.

Many enabled individuals suffer from an addiction, a physical ailment, or a mental health condition. Instead of making steps towards recovery, they became far too comfortable or even started to enjoy being in a position where they had to be taken care of. Due to the overhelping tendencies of the enabler, they are never required to help themselves. In a person suffering from a physical affliction, this may mean they refuse to get up and retrieve things for themselves, even if they are fully capable. Or they may start to expect others to cook for them, even if they have the strength and resources to do so for themselves. Or they may take an extended leave from work, insisting they are too sick or unwell, even if all evidence shows they are perfectly fine.

Since their backgrounds can vary wildly, it is important to examine their childhood. Look at their relationship with their primary caregivers. Were they spoilt in some way or were they outright neglected? Here are some case studies to better help you understand the background of the enabled partner.

Case Studies

To protect the privacy of the people involved, no real names have been used.

- Mary remembers feeling neglected in her childhood. Her little brother suffered from a myriad of health complications as soon as he was brought home from the hospital. Naturally, he got more attention from their parents. She remembers being all alone with her nanny for days at a time while her parents stayed at the hospital with her sick brother. Eventually, her brother got better, but the dynamic was always the same, with him receiving far more attention than her. When she was a teenager, she admits to exaggerating symptoms of an illness because she wanted to get more attention from her parents. This plan succeeded. Suddenly, her parents began giving her the same attention they used to only give her brother. Worried she would become 'ignored' again, she continued to act helpless and sick because she learned that this was the best way to get others to care for her. Eventually, Mary entered a codependent relationship. Her partner went above and beyond to help her because he believed she was very ill and unable to look after herself. To break this codependency, Mary had to learn that there were other more fulfilling ways to receive affection from people.

- For as long as John can remember, he was always given whatever he wanted. He came from an extremely privileged family and he was never required to lift a finger to do anything. He didn't even recognize what a position of privilege he was in; he just thought it was completely normal. If he needed something, there was always a helper available or his parents could easily pay for a solution. In addition to this privilege, he was also an only child with no one to fight over attention for. His mother, in particular, coddled him and he enjoyed being coddled. Eventually, he got into a codependent relationship with a person who grew up taking care of an alcoholic father. Naturally, she became John's enabler. She allowed him to do nothing, taking care of his every need while he took care of financial responsibilities with family money, but nothing else. When they eventually had children, John's partner found herself exhausted and stretched thin. He never helped her with anything and instead still expected her to help him too. Since John was very used to a female enabler being in his life, it was difficult for him to realize that he had deep-set codependent ways.

As demonstrated, enabled partners can be raised in wildly different ways. What they always have in common, however, is that they're taught to equate affection and love with being treated as helpless. In Mary's case, she started to feel that the only way to get attention from her parents was by being sick. In the case of John, he felt that overhelping and being coddled *was* love because of how his parents, especially his mother, treated him. At some point along the way, the lines became blurred with their primary caregiver.

To help the enabled partner in your relationship, see if you can identify where these feelings originated in their childhood. Is your partner more of a Mary or more of a John?

Narcissistic & Borderline Personality Disorder

When dealing with Narcissistic and Borderline Personality Disorder, emotional and psychological abuse are usually at work. Individuals with these personality disorders are always in the enabled position, never the enabler. The codependency becomes infinitely more toxic when these personalities are involved. Narcissists feel entitled to an obedient partner and may even enjoy watching the enabler stumble over them, trying to do everything they can to fulfill their every whim. Indeed, an enabler is a Narcissist's perfect partner. The Narcissist wants to feel special and like the whole world revolves around them, and there the enabler is showing them exactly that. The enabler of a Narcissist is often referred to as a 'Co-Narcissist.'

Borderline personalities can be equally damaging to the enabler; they are prone to feelings of betrayal and abandonment. In the Borderline personality, the enabler sees a victim they can finally save. The Borderline personality wants a hero or savior and it comes naturally for the enabler to play that part. Unfortunately, what the enabler fails to realize is that this is part of the Borderline personality's destructive pattern. They will never truly be the hero in the story because the Borderline will always feel betrayed and abandoned over something. The emotional instability inherent in this personality disorder means the enabler will never succeed in their attempt to save. The Borderline personality has issues that are solely their own problem to solve – the enabler must recognize this as soon as possible.

It is much more difficult for someone with a personality disorder to change. Unless these partners are self-aware and committed to self-transformation, there is a high likelihood they will continue to engage in their usual pattern. And with a Narcissist or Borderline personality, this pattern can be highly destructive. If you're an enabler to one of these personality types, reconsider your involvement in the relationship or invest in couples therapy.

Dependent Personality Disorder

The most common personality disorder found in codependent relationships is – you guessed it – the Dependent Personality Disorder. Those with this personality disorder may fall into either the enabler or enabled position. Dependent personalities are inclined to feel anxiety and fear when they are by themselves. Naturally, they turn to other people to fulfill all their emotional and psychological needs. Without approval, validation, or help from other people, Dependents feel like a fish out of water.

At their most severe, Dependent personalities may have a hard time functioning in their daily lives without something present. This can lead them to shirk responsibilities and become completely passive. When left on their own, they can feel extremely helpless. As you'd expect, Dependent personalities take break-ups harder than the average individual. They may feel utterly devastated until they find someone else to take their ex-partner's place. When an enabler suffers from this disorder, they may be extremely competent while in a relationship but feel there's 'no point' if they don't have someone.

This disorder does not just affect the romantic sphere of the Dependent's life. In fact, everyone who knows the individual will experience their dependency. Friends, family, and perhaps even coworkers and bosses will see this side of the Dependent.

5 Types of Dependent Personalities

Renowned psychologist, Theodore Millon, can be credited with identifying the five distinct types of dependent personalities in adults. While all Dependents will share similar traits, each type will display its own unique behavior and strategies for getting what they want. If you believe either you or your partner have Dependent Personality Disorder, see if you can figure out which type they are. It is possible to have symptoms belonging to a few different types but there is usually just one that dominates.

- The Disquieted Dependent

The Disquieted subtype is wrought with anxiety and restlessness. They fear abandonment from the people around them and feel intense loneliness when they are not with a supportive figure. Feelings of inadequacy run rampant and they are often very sensitive to rejection.

- The Immature Dependent

Dependents under this subtype have a tendency to be childlike, especially in the face of everyday responsibilities. Despite being an adult, they will find it difficult to cope with typical adult expectations. The Immature type needs a significant amount of 'babying' as they can be naive and lacking in general life skills.

- The Accommodating Dependent

This type is characterized by extreme benevolence and, as its name suggests, a tendency to be over-accommodating. These individuals strive to please others and will come across as incredibly agreeable. Naturally, they take on a submissive role and reject all uncomfortable feelings. These types may be very gracious and neighborly towards everyone around them.

- The Selfless Dependent

The Selfless subtype bears many similarities to the Accommodating subtype, but there is a stronger inclination to abandon their individual identity and merge it with another person's. When left unchecked, they'll become absorbed by another person and live as a mere extension of them. Of all the types, these Dependents are most likely to appear as not having a personality.

- The Ineffectual Dependent

Like the Immature Dependent, the Ineffectuals do not cope well with difficulties and responsibilities. The Ineffectuals will take it a step further, however, refusing to deal with anything at all that may be uncomfortable. A caretaker is essential for them to function in life. They are prone to fatigue and lethargy. They are unproductive and most of the time, highly incompetent. On occasion, Ineffectual Dependents may even struggle with feelings of empathy and instead be overcome by a general apathy towards their life, including any shortcomings.

No matter the subtype, all people suffering from this personality disorder can get better with therapy and committed self-work. In fact, many Dependent personalities have found healthy levels of independence after sufficient treatment. If you feel your codependence is linked to this disorder, rest assured that this condition does not have to dictate your life.

Common Wounds of Both Personalities

All dependent personalities may manifest varying behavior, but for the most part, they are rooted in similar psychological wounding. With the exception of some Narcissistic and Borderline Personality types, codependent individuals have low self-esteem and strong insecurities.

At the end of the day, both partners feel they desperately need each other in order to feel complete. The only difference is it takes different types of behavior to achieve this sense of completion – a feeling that never lasts long because it is always up to someone else to fill this need.

By nature, Dependent personalities have trouble forming and distinguishing their own identity. They don't know who they truly are and they have a low sense of personal value. When asked about their core strengths, many will find themselves at a loss for what to say unless they receive feedback from someone else. Their flawed and incomplete sense of identity is exactly why they quickly latch onto other people. They see this other person as a kind of mirror image. Any uncertainty they feel inside is solved by looking to this other person and merging with them.

To eliminate the Dependent's tendency to attach themselves to another person, it is vital that they learn some level of independence. They must experience the world without a crutch to walk on their own. Their family, friends, and partners must learn to give them healthy boundaries and a healthy level of support. Without challenges, they cannot improve and grow into their strength. Codependency is a quick and easy way to placate a deep wound, but it is never a long-term or lasting solution.

Understanding the Anxious Attachment Style

When it comes to understanding one's approach to relationships, attachment styles can shed a lot of light on why certain people behave the way they do. Quite simply, our attachment style shows us how we go about getting what we want and the strategies we use to meet our needs. Our varying approaches are determined by our childhoods, specifically our relationship with our primary caregiver. If you had an emotionally unavailable parent or one that abandoned you in some way, this will affect the way you behave in all future relationships.

The Anxious attachment style is one of three dominant styles and is the one most commonly found in codependent individuals. The Anxious type is formed when an individual experiences trauma during the developmental period of their life. For one reason or another, their 'safe space' was upturned or destroyed. Their sense of physical or emotional safety was compromised in a significant way and it may have resulted in a life-altering breach of trust. This traumatic incident likely involved abandonment, violence, emotional abuse, or other forms of trauma.

As its name suggests, the Anxious type has developed a deep sense of anxiety in response to relationships and intimacy. Whether they show it or not, there is a hypervigilance for signs of abandonment fueled by an intense fear of being left behind in some way. These types crave intimacy and may even fantasize about the 'perfect partner' while single. In relationships, they may resort to manipulation or playing games during times of deep insecurity. They are more inclined to be pessimistic, imagining the worst outcome especially in regards to their close relationships.

The Anxious type is most likely to end up in a codependent relationship because they have a tendency to put their partner's needs before their own. Since abandonment is seen as the worst possible outcome, they naturally strive for the opposite extreme. In the eyes of the Anxious type, codependency is a sign of deep love and unmatched intimacy. The idea of anything less scares them. Codependency allows them to feel like they have 'tabs' on everything happening in the relationship. This is a coping mechanism for their abandonment issues.

The closeness of codependency grants them the illusion of having total control.

The most tight-knit codependencies are formed by two people with this same attachment style. It should be noted, however, that not all people possessing this attachment style will present signs of the same severity. As with everything, all people are on a spectrum. Those with severe Anxious inclinations will need to work harder on breaking their destructive patterns.

At the end of the day, whichever type or attachment style you possess, the lessons that must be learned are the same. If you saw your or your partner's behavior reflected in these pages, don't feel discouraged over getting called out. Just focus on the lessons at hand a nd you'll soon find yourself evolving from your codependent ways.

Chapter 3: For the Love of Boundaries

Whenever the words 'boundaries' or 'limitations' come into the conversation, it is always associated with negative connotations. People tend to think that boundaries will lead to some form of deprivation and that all enjoyment will be stripped from their lives forevermore. This is, of course, a ridiculous notion. Boundaries keep us sane and safe. They are akin to the walls of a house, keeping a healthy barrier between what's ours and what's *out there*. Boundaries and walls don't mean that we live in isolation or loneliness; it simply means we start gaining better control over our thoughts, feelings, and spaces. Without boundaries, the world and our lives would be chaos. Start seeing the beauty in boundaries. Would you want to live in a house with no walls? I'll bet not.

One key thing that all codependents struggle with is – you guessed it! – boundaries. Their tendency to merge identities with another individual means that they no longer embrace their independence. They start to perceive separation and individuality as negative ideas. Boundaries are uncomfortable and difficult to put in place because any separation poses a threat to their peace of mind. They see it as being alone indefinitely instead of healthy and temporary space apart. Whether you realize it or not, your relationship desperately needs boundaries. Avoiding temporary discomfort now could to lasting frustration in the future. Perhaps even a ruined relationship. Many couples who allow this to happen look back in regret, wishing they'd been strong when it mattered the most. Don't let that happen to you and your relationship.

To start healing your codependency, a necessary step is to start working on healthier boundaries and the mindset it takes to make them successful.

5 Vital Ways to Build Strong Self-Awareness

Before boundaries can be established, it's important that you recognize what your needs are and, most importantly, which needs are not currently being met. This requires self-awareness. As a codependent, some of your needs will be difficult to admit to. In fact, you may even find yourself outright disagreeing. Whenever the urges to disagree or fight back arise, consider whether this response is really rooted in your needs or whether you're only reacting out of fear. It is highly common for codependents to fear the challenge of independence. To achieve growth and true happiness, however, it's essential that you embrace this challenge. Self-awareness will keep you grounded and alert about what you need to feel fully satisfied.

1. Write Down Your Thoughts

Try to make a habit of writing down your feelings and thoughts. Notice when an emotion arises and take note of what brings this up. This time to focus on your mind will train you to be more in tune with what you feel and think. Sometimes we don't notice because we never take the time to really experience our inner world. Make sure that whatever you write doesn't fully revolve around your partner. Focus on what *you* feel. Write about other spheres of your life or topics that interest you in the greater world. Feel free to write in a journal or just in a Word document on your computer. Wherever you choose to write, the benefit is the same.

2. Visualize Your Ideal Self

The best part about this exercise is that you can do it anywhere, anytime, and it can take as little as a few minutes. For the best results, however, we advise doing it in the early morning or right before bedtime as this is when your mind is likely to be less agitated. Close your eyes and start to form a mental picture of your future self. What does your ideal self look like? What has he or she accomplished that you're proud of? What are your ideal self's biggest strengths? How does he or she act in the face of life's challenges? Now, imagine that this ideal self is actually who you're looking at in the mirror. You already are your ideal self. Embrace the strengths you wish to have. They are already in you waiting to be unlocked.

Not only does this exercise empower you but it also allows you to see what your true values are. And most importantly, it allows you to reconnect with your dreams and your purpose. Needless to say, while performing this exercise, it's important that you keep all your visualizations strictly about you and not involved with your partner.

3. Ask Someone for Feedback

The thought of asking someone for feedback can seem terrifying but it's one of the best ways to receive an honest insight. Make sure to choose someone who knows you reasonably well and whose opinion you trust. Also, make sure whoever you talk to will be capable of staying constructive. Steer clear of anyone in your life who is overly critical or unkind. You can do this in person, over the phone or even by email. Ask this person what they feel your strengths are and where they think your areas for growth are. When you receive that feedback, think it over. Embrace your strengths and also look at your areas for growth in a level-headed, practical manner. When moving forward with your personal growth, try and work on these areas the best you can.

4. Take Different Personality Tests

Whether it's the Myers-Briggs test, a SWOT analysis, or an Enneagram quiz, try and have fun with some different personality tests. The goal here is to get to know yourself a little better and solidify your sense of self. Not only will these tests give you new insights into your personality attributes, they will also point out strengths you may have never considered before. Identifying your Myers-Briggs and Enneagram type will aid you in putting your needs into words, and they'll give you a much better idea of where you'll need to set some boundaries. If you discover that you're deeply introverted, you may realize that alone time and solitude is very important to you. Or perhaps it's the opposite and you realize it's more social time with friends that you desperately need in your life. Take these newly identified needs into account and plan on making them a priority in your brand new non-codependent chapter.

5. Monitor Your Inner Dialogue

Every single person engages in self-talk and, even if we don't realize, we are strongly influenced by the manner in which we speak to ourselves. Pay attention to your inner dialogue when faced with different events and decisions. When you do something wrong, what does the voice in your head say? When you do something right, do you give yourself the positive encouragement you deserve or do you give someone else the credit? Take note of the patterns in your inner dialogue. Notice when you're being harsh on yourself.

Instead of putting yourself down for failures, try to be constructive and show yourself compassion. If you can, think of a solution instead of a put-down. If you forgot to pay your phone bill again, don't dwell on your forgetfulness. Be kind to yourself; perhaps you've been stressed or working hard at something else. What can you do to prevent this from happening in the future? Perhaps, you could create reminders on your phone or leave brightly colored post-it notes on the fridge. Try dwelling on the solution instead of the problem.

"So, Where Exactly Should I Draw the Line?"

Using the ideas in the previous section, you might have come up with a few ideas for boundaries you can set. I highly encourage you to run with these and make them happen! If you still don't have any clear ideas, don't worry. You're codependent and you may not be accustomed to thinking in terms of yourself yet. Here are some ideas for where you can draw some boundaries:

1. Time Together

In codependent relationships, it's very common for both partners to spend an exorbitant amount of time together. This is a good place to start when you're thinking of where to draw boundaries. If you see each other everyday, suggest spending one or two days apart to focus on your individual hobbies. If you live together, this may mean taking the day out in different areas and only seeing each other in the evenings. If it isn't realistic to spend whole days apart, consider modifying your daily routine so you spend a few hours in a secluded area of the house.

2. Household Chores

It's very common for the enabler to take on most of the household chores. They are, after all, the more active partners in the relationship. A great way to establish more balance in your dynamic is by adding more fairness to your household duties. This aspect of living with a partner is easily overlooked but it is a huge signifier of balance or imbalance in the relationship. If you tend to do most or all of the chores, tell your partner you will no longer bear most of the burden. Insist on doing half of the chores each. If you're inclined to be more gentle on them, you could even let them choose which chores they would prefer to do. Make sure you stick to this new arrangement by giving them frequent reminders or putting up a chore roster.

3. Bad Habits

This is a big one in codependent relationships. The enabled partners always have some bad habit that is creating strain in the relationship. It could be something as major as a drug addiction or something less major like general laziness. Drawing boundaries around bad habits is essential in a codependent relationship, especially if it's affecting you in some way. Be firm with this boundary, but also think of ways you can support them through this boundary. If you need your partner to go to AA meetings, consider being the person to drive them to each meeting. If you want your partner to get a job, help them look for jobs and put together a dazzling resume. If there are little habits that bother you, consider drawing boundaries there as well. Don't like it when your partner leaves his dirty socks on the sofa? Start setting that boundary!

4. Verbal Communication: Language & Tone

Verbal communication is a difficult one to master and it's possible your partner has tendencies that really irk you. Maybe even more than that – maybe you find them hurtful and upsetting. If your partner speaks to you in a way that you find bothersome, don't hesitate to call it out, especially if they call you names, raise their voice, mock you, or belittle you in moments of anger. Boundaries around counterproductive communication styles can be more difficult to implement since these decisions are made in the spur of the moment, but I'm willing to bet that until now you haven't fought back. Just calling it out and telling your partner you will no longer tolerate it can be enough to put a stop to it.

5. Decisions and Making Plans

If one person in your relationship consistently takes on a dominant role, it's likely that person makes most of the decisions. Some of these may include what activities to partake in, what to eat, where to go, and who to see. If your partner tends to get his or her way when it comes to making plans, try and point this fact out. Draw boundaries around how often they can dominate your shared plans. Suggest sharing this decision or allocating certain days to your choice and your partner's choice. And if it's you that tends to dominate, have the strength to create this balance in your relationship. If your partner shrugs the decision off and asks you to choose every single time, insist that they choose. They may be hesitant but later on, knowing they made this decision will empower them in their own life.

6. How to Spend Money

This decision is another big one. A lack of boundaries around finances can lead to a lot of resentment for couples who don't learn to work together. In a codependent relationship, there's a high likelihood one partner is spending more money than the other or putting it towards something that is destructive to their own lifestyle. Perhaps you have a partner that is spending all your money on shopping and you just can't say no. Or perhaps he or she is using it to pay for their bad habits. If money is going towards a counterproductive activity or habit, start drawing boundaries here. There are always better things to invest in. Bring up your future together. Think of all the money you could have saved for a new house, a new TV, or even a vacation together. Come together to draw boundaries on how money gets spent and how much; you won't regret it!

4 Questions to Eliminate Guilt Before Setting Boundaries

Whenever codependent partners are faced with the thought of boundary-setting, they inevitably bring up the guilt they feel. This all goes back to the unhealthy notion that boundaries are unkind. Codependent people feel that this is equivalent to slapping their partner's hand away or telling them to back off. Let's clear this up right now: boundary-setting is not rejection! When done properly, no feelings are hurt and everyone wins. A lack of boundaries can lead to people feeling resentment or frustration down the road – and this can do real damage to a romantic partnership.

While it's completely normal for codependent people to have hesitation about setting boundaries, they need to recognize this feeling must be overcome. If the thought of setting boundaries with your partner makes you feel uncomfortable, that's okay! This is just further proof that you really are codependent. The good news is this guilt can be eliminated with some self-reflection. Now, let's get working!

- "How is my lack of boundaries holding me back from my dreams and goals?

After utilizing the suggestions in the 'Self-Awareness' section, think about the path between where you are now and the goals you want to achieve. Whether you realize it or not, your lack of boundaries is creating an obstacle. How exactly does this obstacle manifest itself? This doesn't have to be your big life dream, it can also be your short-term goals. For example, let's say you've been wanting to start working out so you can get in better shape. If you aren't creating boundaries around money and time, this leaves less available to achieve this goals. If you're buying your codependent partner anything he or she wants, and spending every minute of every day with them, how are you going to afford a membership at a great gym? How will you find the time or energy to start working out? Reflect on how satisfying it would be to finally achieve these goals. Wouldn't it be a shame if you let your relationship get in the way? How will you feel later on in life when you realize your chance is over?

- "In what ways will I feel more positive after I set these boundaries?"

Imagine how it'll feel after you successfully set these boundaries. You don't have to name these feelings if you don't want to. Just experience it mentally and emotionally. Try to put yourself in the shoes of your future self. It could be a few weeks or months down the road – whenever your boundaries have been able to reap their full benefits. If you're setting boundaries to get more time to yourself, think of all the things you'll accomplish with that time. Imagine how it'll make you feel to see how much you've achieved because you had the strength to set those boundaries. If you're considering adding more rules to the way money is spent, imagine having all that extra money in the future. What will you do with it? Think of the many wonderful things you can put your saved money towards! Imagine taking a fantastic vacation with your partner because you were finally able to restrict their terrible spending habits!

- "In what ways will my partner grow if I set these boundaries?"

You think you're helping by not drawing boundaries, but this could not be further from the truth. Let's examine that flawed belief for a moment. What exactly makes you think you're helping by letting them do as they please? Is it because in that moment you're not causing them discomfort or displeasure? Why is short-term displeasure the enemy and not long-term frustration or dissatisfaction? People grow through challenges. As a partner, it's not your job to eliminate all challenges;

it's your job to make sure your partner has the necessary support through their life challenges. Support means staying by their side not sacrificing your well-being.

What will your partner improve through these new boundaries? How will they grow? If you're trying to help your partner quit a bad habit, think of the growth they'll see once they finally let it go. Perhaps they'll have better health, more money, and more time to focus on their goals. They may learn to be more patient, more empowered, and they may even start to be a better partner towards you.

- "How will my relationship be stronger after better boundaries?"

With the answers to all the other questions in mind, reflect on the overall impact these boundaries will have on your relationship. You've now identified the ways in which you will feel more positive and the growth your partner will see; what does this mean for your relationship as a whole? Your relationship may be comfortable now, but what if your relationship was empowering instead? Imagine what you'd be able to accomplish together.

Essential Tips for Setting Healthy Boundaries Successfully

1. Add Boundaries as Seamlessly As Possible

Here's a pro tip for setting boundaries with positive outcomes: weave them in seamlessly and do not make a big deal out of them. A rookie mistake that new boundary-setters make is approaching the topic with a heavy, sad air and infusing too much intensity into the conversation. There's no need to treat it this way! If want to reserve a day each week for working out, just say, "Hey honey, I'm going to start focusing on getting fit. I've been dying to get in shape! I'm thinking of making Saturday my solo work-out day. You're going to love my new hot bod - just wait!" Notice how casual and lighthearted this is. By bringing new changes up this way, it doesn't feel scary and serious. It's just a small new change - no big deal! Your partner is less likely to worry and you'll see for yourself how incredibly normal it sounds to draw boundaries.

2. Use Positive Language

If you're trying to suggest more time apart, do *not* say, "Darling, I think we need to spend more time apart. It's driving me crazy and I can't handle it anymore." This negative and emotional language will worry your partner. Remind yourself that this isn't a negative event, it's quite the opposite. Your relationship is evolving. Be positive and excited for your new chapter. If you're discussing your new boundaries with your partner, infuse the conversation with positive language. Focus on the benefits you'll see instead of how difficult it's going to be.

3. Assure Your Partner

Needless to say, the first conversation you have about boundaries may incite a little bit of anxiety in your partner. Expect this and don't let it discourage you. When it happens, assure and remind your partner that the reason you want these boundaries is because you want to improve your relationship. Why? Because you love your partner and you want to ensure both your happiness for the future to come. When your partner appears worried, continue to bring up this fact. Inaction is a greater signifier of our apathy in a relationship; if you're actively trying to make improvements, this is evidence that you really care about the future of your relationship.

4. Stay Firm & Do Not Waver

Since boundaries are new to your relationship, it's possible that there will be some pushback from your partner. Prepare in advance for how you'll respond. Whatever you do, stay firm in your assertions and do not back down. If you appear ambivalent or uncertain, this will only add to your partner's hesitation. Remain confident and you'll eventually convince your partner that this is the best course of action. If your partner is prone to manipulation or guilt-tripping, make further preparations for these tactics. See if you can guess how they'll resist and come up with an effective comeback. Keep the benefits of your boundaries in mind and do not allow them to pull you back into your old destructive patterns.

5. Do Not Make Threats

If your partner disrespects the boundaries you've aligned, it's important that there are some consequences for this – but only handle this outcome when it occurs. Do not make threats in anticipation of this event. For the moment, try to believe that your partner will take these boundaries seriously. As soon as threats enter the conversation, you start veering off into emotionally abusive territory. It is absolutely essential that your partner starts making changes out of love for you and your relationship, and not fear for the consequences you've threatened them with. Threatening them will infuse a lot of negativity into the situation and it will only worsen the codependence.

6. Emphasize Change on Both Sides

If you want your partner to cooperate, avoid making it sound like they are the only person who needs to change. Remember, you're both co-creating this situation. As we established in the previous chapter, it takes two personalities to form codependency. Even if you feel like your partner has more work to do, it's important that you take accountability for your actions as well. Tell them what you're going to do as your part in this new change. Your partner will be far more likely to respond positively if you make it sound like this is a journey you're embarking on together. Do not pin the responsibility solely on them.

7.   Abide by Your Own Rules

If you're going to draw boundaries in your relationship then you, too, must respect them. How can you expect your partner to take them seriously if you don't? It is completely unfair to ask your partner to change and then not do your own self-work. If you're trying to restrict your partner's drug habit, then it's only fair you control your alcohol dependence. A good rule of thumb is to treat every boundary you create for your partner as a boundary for yourself as well. Do not be a hypocrite. Keep the playing field level at all times and listen to your own rules. You help to set the tone for how seriously your boundaries can be taken.

Chapter 4: Developing Powerful Self-Esteem

The overall health of a relationship is dependent on the two individuals belonging to it. It is not its own entity. If you're a deeply insecure person, you're going to carry those insecurities into your relationship. If you're jealous while you're single, you're going to be a jealous partner as well. These issues don't just disappear as soon as someone else is in the picture. Expecting a relationship to fix you is another way that codependency forms. Partners cling to each other with hopes it'll diminish their inner turmoil, led to believe it's the ultimate cure. When it doesn't seem to work, they cling harder until the attempt backfires entirely. To be in a healthy relationship, you need to work on being a healthy individual. One way to do this is by working on your self-esteem. Believe it or not, broken self-esteem is often the root of many flawed relationship dynamics. This is no less true for codependencies. The tips and exercises in this chapter will all contribute to a stronger sense of self and more powerful self-esteem. Take the time out to think of you and only you.

How High Self-Esteem Can Improve Your Codependency

Codependent partners tend to be in denial about the connection between self-esteem and codependency. Many insist that their codependency is born out of deep love and commitment for each other, but this is a delusion. Deep love and commitment may indeed exist but many couples are able to feel the same way without resorting to unhealthy patterns. One of the major differences is that healthy couples have higher levels of self-esteem. These are the improvements self-esteem can make to daily dynamics:
Example #1

Low Self-Esteem: You frequently doubt yourself and feel indecisive. This results in inaction about how to go about reaching your goals. You're not even sure if they're good goals to have. Overall, you feel overwrought with skepticism about your choices in life. This is why you rely on your partner to tell you what to do.

High Self-Esteem: When it comes to your goals, you trust that you can find the right course of action. This doesn't mean you won't make any mistakes along the way, but you trust that if you do, you'll discover how to fix the problem and do so accordingly. You listen to your partner's feedback but you never allow it to be the deciding vote, unless you agree.

Example #2

Low Self-Esteem: It feels like you do everything wrong. Every time you try to do something new, it always backfires and fails. You don't believe you have any strong abilities. You prefer it if your partner does everything because you can't do anything as well as they can. You believe yourself to be deeply incompetent.

High Self-Esteem: You may not do everything right all the time, but you know you're still a highly competent person. There's a learning curve for everyone and you always get it right eventually. You are completely comfortable taking care of your own self and are happy to share chores or other tasks with your partner since you know you can handle them just as well. No one's perfect but you know you can do anything you put your mind to.

Example #3

Low Self-Esteem: You're so afraid of being by yourself. This is why you can't implement any boundaries in your relationship; you're terrified it will cause your partner to leave you. Even when your partner does something that bothers you, you bite your tongue and keep your feelings to yourself. You just want to please them so that they stay with you. You don't know who you are without them and you're not sure how you'd go on by yourself. You desperately need them in your life to feel secure.

High Self-Esteem: Of course you love your partner - after all, that's why you're with them! - but you'll be okay if your relationship doesn't work out. You're in the relationship because you want your partner, not because you *need* your partner. You have no problem being honest and setting boundaries with your partner because you know what you need to be happy in a relationship. If your partner isn't willing to cooperate then that's a clear sign they aren't the right person for you. You know your worth and value outside of being in a couple. Your relationship consists of two whole people – not two halves.

Quit Codependency with these 22 Self-Esteem Affirmations

Positive affirmations are a proven way to improve one's self-talk. By reciting empowering mantras, your inner dialogue shifts and all self-sabotaging tendencies can be relinquished over time. To help build your self-esteem and solidify your inner confidence, try and make these positive affirmations part of your self-talk. Continued practice will rewire your brain to instantly feel more personal satisfaction.

1. Everything I need is already inside of me.
2. I am the master of my own emotions.
3. Today I will overcome obstacles with renewed strength.

4. I am my own fortress. I, alone, am in control of what enters and what leaves.
5. I can easily supply whatever I need.
6. I am capable of doing great things.
7. I let go of my past troubles and welcome brighter days.
8. I can stand proudly and courageously on my own.
9. I am open and ready to experience my true power.
10. Every step I take leads me to success.
11. I am fueled by my inner magic.
12. I am inhaling powerful confidence and exhaling self-doubt.
13. I am stronger than ever before.
14. I am whole and I am enough.
15. I am buzzing with brilliance.
16. Everything I touch becomes infused with light.
17. I am an unstoppable force.
18. I am an overflowing cup of love and joy.
19. I am fire and I am blazing ahead.
20. The universe supports me and all of my dreams.
21. Beauty is all around me and I create it wherever I go.
22. Today is the beginning of my best life chapter so far.

8 Exercises for Developing Powerful Self-Esteem

The greatest thing about self-esteem is that it can be built. How you feel about yourself now is not how you'll feel forever. The only reason you have low self-esteem is because your brain is used to creating negative thoughts about yourself – but it is in no way indicative of who you really are. It's time to break the pattern for good and start looking at yourself with kindness. You possess many positive qualities and it's time you start recognizing that.

1. The Journal of Wins

Your days are filled with wins. You may not realize it, but it's true. The reason you don't notice them is because you're waiting for a big win to fall out from the sky, but you accomplish small and medium wins every single day! These deserve to be celebrated too. Thing is, it isn't realistic to accomplish a big win every day. No one does that! To rev yourself up for a big win, start a journal and fill it with your little victories. Every day, list three things that you did right – both the intentional and unintentional wins. Did you make yourself an absolutely delicious sandwich? Did you spend less time on social media today than you did yesterday? Perhaps you gave a stranger a compliment and it made them noticeably happy? These are all wins to be celebrated!

2. Blame the Circumstances, Not the Individual

Whenever we make a mistake, we have a tendency to blame our personality. This isn't always fair. The next time you fail or make a mistake, try blaming the circumstances instead. For example, let's say you forgot to pick up groceries on your way home from work. Instead of calling yourself forgetful or stupid, try calling out the circumstances that got you here. Attribute this mistake to how busy you've been lately and the stress you've been feeling. You would have remembered to do the task if you weren't so tired! It's not who you are deep down inside. Now, it's important to not dwell on the mistake. Start thinking of solutions for next time, should the same circumstances arise.

3. Talk to Someone that Makes You Feel Great

How we feel about ourselves is strongly influenced by the people we're around. If you spend a lot of time with people who speak negatively about you or the world in general, you're going to absorb this negativity into your self-talk. If you can't eliminate everyone that makes you feel bad about yourself, make a point to also spend time with people that make you feel great. Spend time with them without bringing your partner along, if you can. Do they make you feel funny? Smart? Capable? Insightful? Lean into these good feelings and have fun with your new friend. And recognize that you truly are all these wonderful qualities that you feel!

4. Get Physical

Getting physical may sound like an odd way to build self-esteem but believe it or not, it works wonders. When we go on a hike or jog a couple of miles, we are faced with real evidence of our ability to accomplish something. We are simply doing and then succeeding. When we sit and stew in our own thoughts, it's easy for negativity and self-doubt to come flooding in. We need to get in the habit of simply *doing* and then looking back to see how far we've come. When we get active, we can put a distance to our progress or admire the view from our goal. It's a great way to remind ourselves of our power because we are *using* our power to give ourselves proof! The endorphins from getting active and the chance to remove yourself from your routine will also give you an immediate mood boost.

5. Respond to the Devil on your Shoulder

Some of us have an on-going relationship with the devil on our shoulder. It doesn't matter what we do, there's always a little voice telling us we're still not good enough. This voice may even convince us to stay away from any possible risk because we'll fail or we don't have the abilities to succeed. You've likely heard this voice before. However, I'll bet you normally listen and keep quiet when you hear it. From now on, you will not let this voice get away with making you feel bad. Even if it makes you feel crazy, respond to the devil on your shoulder. Fight, if necessary. Ask him what evidence he has to support what he's saying and throw conflicting evidence back at him. Think of how someone close to you would stick up for you in this situation.

6. Stand in a Power Pose

In a recent study, it was discovered that participants who stood in a power pose saw a decrease in their stress levels and an increase in their level of testosterone (which determines confidence). This is no surprise, of course, as body language is a known way of influencing our own state of mind. The next time you feel disempowered, sad, or low-energy, get yourself into one of these power poses for at least two minutes:

- Stand proudly with your legs apart and hands placed firmly on your hips. Make sure to push out your chest and straighten your back.
- Lean back in your chair and put your feet up on the table. Keep your hands folded behind your head and open out your chest.
- Lean back in your chair with your legs spread apart. Drape one arm over something that is next to you (such as a chair) feel free to do whatever you like with the other arm.

Try and avoid low-power poses by steering clear of crossing your arms, folding your hands, or hunching over in your seat. These will have the reverse effect. Choose a power pose and do it now!

7. Create an Alter Ego

Using an alter ego is a proven method for raising your confidence. In a study on mixed martial arts fighters, it was found that their creation of an alter ego helped to make them feel and perform better in the ring. Think of all the qualities you admire and start constructing a character that embodies all of these qualities. You can even think of a name for this character, if you like. The next time you're in a scenario where you feel shy or insecure, play this character. Ask yourself what this character would say if they were in this position and consider what they would do, how they would behave, etc. If you're taking this character out in public, try to not use their false name or give them a whole new life as it may be awkward if people find out you've been pretending. Make sure it's still you, but the 2.0 version of you. For a little extra fun, you can even play pretend that this character has a superpower. But this time, it's very important you don't try to show it off in public!

8. Treat Yourself Like a Loved One

The next time you catch yourself speaking negatively about who you are or what you've done, I want you to hold those thoughts. Now, instead of saying them to yourself, I want you to think of saying them to someone that you love. How would you feel if you heard someone speak that way to your loved ones? If it makes you feel angry or upset, this is the correct response. This should show you that negative self-talk is not the right way to talk to yourself either. If you want to give yourself criticism, think of how you'd give criticism to someone you really care about. You'd make it constructive and gentle, wouldn't you? Perhaps, you'd even take the time to remind them of their strengths. Imagine forming this constructive criticism for someone else and vow to only criticize yourself in this same gentle way.

Another alternative to this exercise is imagining your negative self-talk being directed at your child self. Do you know what you looked like when you were a little kid? A toddler, even? Can you imagine speaking so negatively to that small child? I'll bet you'd instantly start to feel bad. Again, form criticism as if you'd be speaking to this child self. This is the only right way to criticize yourself.

Chapter 5: Breaking Destructive Patterns

Codependent partners put up with a lot from each other and sometimes this includes a lot of destructive tendencies. Due to the clinging and enabling nature of codependencies, these habits and patterns are rarely dealt with in a proper manner. When the primary goal revolves around making your partner stay no matter what, a lot of problematic behavior gets swept under the rug. Then, denial sets in. Partners get too comfortable in the existing dynamic – so comfortable that incredibly unhealthy behavior is allowed to become normal. Chances are that your relationship, too, is filled with bad habits that need to be broken. You may not even be aware of their impact and the role they play in fueling the toxicity of your relationship. It doesn't matter how much work you do on your mentality; if your actions don't reflect that evolved mentality, it defeats the entire purpose of the self-work. There's no better time than now to end your destructive patterns.

5 Ways to Defeat Intense Jealousy

The clinging nature of a codependent relationship means that both partners, naturally, are afraid of the other person leaving them. This can often result in intense jealousy. One or both partners will look at people who they deem potential lovers of their significant other with heightened scrutiny. There's no telling who these 'potential lovers' will be identified as but whoever they are, the jealous partner will pull their significant other in the opposite direction. When jealousy is on overdrive, this can result in the isolation of both partners, since this is the only way they can assure their protection from individuals who make them jealous.

When jealousy and possessiveness are at their worst, there can also be jealousy over absolutely anyone that's close to the significant other in question. This can be friends and sometimes even family. The jealous partner feels the intense need to be the only one and does not want their 'special' closeness to be rivalled in any way. Needless to say, jealousy in any form can lead to destructive behavior, if left unchecked. While fleeting moments of jealousy are normal, they are considered serious when partners start taking action due to their jealousy. This can be anything like stalking this person on social media or trying to limit their time with our partner. Nip jealousy in the bud before it tears your relationship apart.

1. What if Your Roles Were Reversed?

During times of jealousy, we're essentially trying to guess how our partner feels in that moment. We don't have any facts, just uninformed guesses fueled by our insecurities. We're so hung up on thinking of our partner as a distant 'other' that we forget the terrible outcome we're imagining doesn't make that much sense.

Let's say you're at a party and there's an attractive person in the room. You suspect your partner is attracted to them and your mind is swarmed by awful thoughts where they leave you for this other person. Instead of continuing to picture this awful scenario, I want you to imagine a reverse scenario. What if there was an attractive person in the room that you were attracted to? What would be going through your head? How likely do you think it would be that you'd consider running off with this person and leaving your partner? Would you instantly forget your partner right then and there? The answer is probably no. What's more realistic is you'd notice this attractive person for a moment and then you'd move on with your life. This is most likely how it is for your partner as well. The next time you find yourself feeling jealous, ask yourself how you'd act if your roles were reversed.

2. Use Your Great Imagination to Your Advantage

Jealous people usually have fantastic imaginations. With very little information they can go off into their own little world and imagine the absolute worst outcome. The next time you catch yourself imagining the worst, I want you to try the opposite. I want you to use your imagination to think of the best case scenario instead. There's no reason this would be less likely than the worst case scenario! If your partner has an attractive coworker and you're imagining them falling in love while they work on a project together, stop right there and flip it around. Imagine your partner instead looking at this person and thinking about how much better looking you are. This may be the moment they realize 'Wow, I must really be in love with my partner because even though this other person is objectively attractive, I'm not attracted to him/her." What if, instead, your partner spends the whole time talking about you? These possibilities are just as likely. Why does it always have to be the worst?

3. Talk to Your Partner

Sometimes there's no better solution than just talking it out. Be honest with your partner and tell them how you feel about this other person. Jealous people jump to the worst conclusions and it's only when they hear their partner's feedback that they realize what a ridiculous assumption it was. Your partner may be able to clear up that no, he wasn't staring at that person because he was checking them out, he just thought that they looked an awful lot like their cousin. You never know until you bring it up. Your partner will reassure you that everything is alright and you'll quickly have your jealous feelings resolved. Only do this when your jealousy is really bothering you though, and avoid bringing it up every single time. Whenever you can, you should try and handle your thoughts on your own. Don't rely on your partner to fix everything for you.

4. Accept that Attraction is Normal

You could have the most loyal partner in the world who worships the ground you walk on – even this person is going to find some other people attractive. That's just how we're biologically wired. Attraction is completely normal. You can't stop it. As difficult as it is, you'll need to come to terms with this reality. Instead of feeling hurt by this human impulse, see if you can modify your psyche to just see it as a normal occurrence. Everyone feels attraction. Attraction is not a choice, it is just another feeling like hot, cold, hungry, or thirsty. Feelings of attraction are not the same as love and they are certainly not the same as cheating. As long as your partner isn't being disrespectful, it's no reason to punish them.

5. Remind Yourself that Feelings are Different from Actions

Jealous people get hung up on attraction like it's the same thing as cheating or flirting – but this could not be further from the truth. As we established in the previous point, attraction is a normal impulse. When you find yourself resenting your partner over their possible attraction towards someone, remind yourself that this is not an action they are taking. There's a difference between feeling hungry and gorging yourself on a feast. Someone might be thirsty but that's not the same as downing a jug of beer. Remind yourself that your partner hasn't taken any actions so there's no reason to feel upset or jealous.

6. Recognize that Your Feelings are a Reflection of You, Not Them

What people fail to realize is that their feelings about others are not indicative of anyone else's reality. Your jealousy is, in fact, a reflection of your own inner reality and your own insecurities. If you wish you were taller, you'll be jealous of tall people when, in fact, your

53

partner may not care at all about this factor. A key step to defeating jealousy is to come to terms with this fact. Your feelings say more about you than anyone else. If you get hung up on an idea, it's likely to be more reflective of your insecurities as opposed to your partner's actual sense of attraction to someone else.

How to Break the Pattern of Narcissistic Abuse

As we established in an earlier chapter, many narcissists end up in codependent relationships. Narcissists enjoy finding an enabler and unfortunately, many take pleasure in making them bend to their every whim. If you're currently in a codependent relationship with a narcissist or recovering from one, then there's a chance you've suffered through narcissistic abuse. Before we start breaking the pattern, it's important you understand how the narcissist cycle works:

- STAGE ONE - The Pedestal

When a narcissist is getting what they want or pleased with the way you treat them, they'll respond by putting you on a pedestal. At this stage, it can almost be difficult to believe the narcissist is truly a narcissist. They'll come across as sweet and loving, perhaps even attentive, as they try their best to conceal their dark side. For a short time, you'll feel as though you're on top of the world, like your narcissist partner really cherishes you. It's important to remember that they're only being so nice to you because they're getting what they want. Their goal is to encourage you to continue giving them what they want.

- STAGE TWO - The 'Betrayal'

As soon as the narcissist stops getting *exactly* their way, you'll see a completely different side of them. They may start to feel victimized, threatened or just outright offended. Often times, the trigger may seem completely harmless, though you'll start to recognize common triggers each time. It all comes down to what threatens their view that they are the center of the world. This can vary slightly with each narcissist. This perceived betrayal will push them into attack mode and can lead to much verbal abuse, lying, manipulation, accusations, and other forms of emotional abuse. This is where the narcissist is at his or her worst, actively trying to dominate and force the other person into submission.

- STAGE THREE - The Discard

How the narcissist acts at this stage depends on the response they receive in stage two. If they find it acceptable, they'll stop being aggressive. Instead, there may be mind games like the silent treatment. Without being aggressive or overt, the narcissist will start planting the seeds for stage one again. If the narcissist is not pleased with how you responded to them (and sometimes there's no telling what will trigger this) they will discard you, all for not putting up with their terrible behavior. They'll do this while making you out to be the villain while they're, of course, the victim. It doesn't matter how reasonable you are at this point, the narcissist is set on making a dramatic exit. Partners who aren't yet accustomed to the cycle will find this stage very heartbreaking as they may think they are losing the narcissist for good.

- STAGE FOUR - The Return

If you give the narcissist an opening, they'll come crawling back. Once they're done stirring up drama, the narcissist will try and pretend that they never did or said anything terrible. They'll hope that you, too, will try to let it slide. If you forgive them and allow them to get away with what they did, you'll start back over at stage one, where the narcissist will begin showering you in affection again. This final stage is crucial as it determines whether the cycle continues or if it finally gets better from here. It is at this point that the enabler of the narcissist should think about setting down some real rules.

Now that we've established the four stages of the narcissist cycle, we can finally work on the essential lessons all enablers must learn.

1. Understand that You're in Charge of Breaking the Cycle

Make no mistake, if you want to change the way this cycle plays out, it's up to you to take action and demand improvements. The narcissist will not make any changes on their own. They will continue on the same path because it has always worked for them. They do not have a high enough level of empathy to change on their own for the sake of your happiness. Their priority is getting what they want and they will believe this is the correct way until you show them it no longer works. The narcissist will not change – so you must.

2. Never Blame Yourself

Even though your demands are in charge of breaking the cycle, this doesn't mean you should blame yourself if it goes wrong. When your narcissist displays abusive behavior, it is never your fault. Hold them accountable for their decisions. As soon as you take the fall for something that is not your mistake, the narcissist will feel they have won. They will feel victorious in that moment and worse yet, this will encourage them to misbehave in the future. If they know you'll blame yourself and let them get off scot-free, they will continue down this upsetting path. If they made the choice, they alone should hold the blame.

3. Vow to Make Sure Every Violation is Punished

Always remember that narcissists just want to get their way. Teach them that abuse will only get them further away from their desire. Whenever they do or say anything hurtful, punish them by withdrawing from the situation. Before you do, let them know you are angry and that you will not cooperate in any way if they are resorting to abuse. Show them that as soon as abuse enters the conversation, you are not participating. Removal from the situation is usually the best course of action since some narcissists find pleasure in big displays of emotion. To them, this means you care and this emotion can be used against you. Even if the narcissist says something mildly insulting, they'll begin to learn that even this is unacceptable if you stop allowing them to get away with it.

4. Call Them Out on Everything

Using the narcissist cycle detailed above, keep an eye on which stage your narcissist is in at all times. Whenever you notice them making a power move or trying to manipulate the situation in any way, call them out on it. This is frustrating to the narcissist because they always think they're outsmarting the people around them. If you let them know you're aware of their tactics, this will show them their usual methods don't work. By pointing out their manipulative ways, you can corner them into being more honest with you.

5. Understand that Stage Two is Unavoidable

Unfortunately, there's no way to avoid the perceived betrayal when you're dealing with the narcissist. Unless, of course, you plan on letting them do whatever they want at all times. While you can't steer clear of their strong emotions, you can help them find better ways to express these emotions. Ideally, these improved ways should not involve any form of abuse. If the narcissist is having a bad day, then always do what you can to protect yourself from the fallout of stage two. If you're in a fragile place, you may want to get away for a while and turn your phone off. Or perhaps meditate before you decide to talk to them.

6. Implement Stronger Boundaries at Stage Four

The narcissist has some time to calm down at stage three, so by the time stage four rolls around, try and put down some stronger boundaries. This is the stage where the cycle ends and begins all over again. If you want to start with a healthier dynamic, make this clear to the narcissist once the big explosion has finally settled. It is at this point that the narcissist will be most likely to absorb what you're saying. If you're not sure what boundaries to set, consider the following questions: what was the trigger this time? What abusive or unhealthy responses did they display when they became upset? What did you feel most hurt by? Draw boundaries around their abusive behavior and discuss healthier ways they can let their grievances be known. Be clear about what behaviors you find unacceptable at stage two and be firm about how there will be consequences next time.

7. Know that Attachment or Addiction is Not the Same as Love

If you're in a relationship with an abusive narcissist, consider seeking professional help or leaving the situation, especially if you think your emotional well-being is at stake. Unless the narcissist is committed to improving their ways, it is highly unlikely that they'll make lasting changes for the better. Enablers often stay with their narcissist partners as they're convinced the narcissist will change if they just stick around a little longer. Unfortunately, this results in a lot of wasted time and even more hurt feelings. The enablers will always claim to have a deep love for the narcissist - and in some cases, this may be true - but more often than not, the narcissist just has them hooked. Intermittent reinforcement (the cycle of showing love, pulling it away, then giving it back) is scientifically proven to create feelings that mimic addiction. Often enablers are so hooked to the rollercoaster cycle of the narcissist that they mistake this attachment for love. It's extremely important that you make the distinction between these two different feelings.

The 10 Terrible Habits You Need to Quit Immediately

1. Asking Where Your Partner is at All Times

It's normal to have check-ins with your partner but many codependent people take this to a new level. Every hour to every couple of hours, the codependent couple will feel the need to ask the other partner where they are. What sets this behavior apart from the check-ins of non-codependent couples is the frequency with which they happen and the attitude behind them. When codependent couples check in with each other, there tends to be anxiety behind their questioning. They aren't just curious but they *need* to know. The next time you're apart from your partner, see if you can keep check-ins limited to once every four or five hours at the very least.

2. Looking Through Your Partner's Phone

A surprising number of people are guilty of snooping through their partner's phone. Having done it once or twice is not a big deal but it should *never* become a habit. If you need to look through your partner's devices to get peace of mind, your relationship needs a lot of work. If either partner is worried or anxious, the solution should always be to bring it up with your partner so you can cooperate on the basis of trust. If you can't do this, you should learn to let it go by developing the appropriate detachment tools. Snooping through someone's phone is a violation of privacy, no matter how discreet. A major step towards breaking codependency is learning to respect each other's personal space. Stop snooping!

3. Inviting Your Partner to Every Hangout with Friends

There's absolutely nothing wrong bringing your partner into your friend circle. In fact, some of the best times to be had are likely to come about when this happens. No matter how much fun it is, you should always make sure to get some alone time with your friends. To continue having happy and fulfilling friendships, the initial bond should be nurtured – and this doesn't involve your partner. Your friends may not tell you but they, too, wish they could have you alone sometimes. The dynamic changes once someone's significant other is in the room, and although this dynamic may still be fun, there's nothing like getting quality time the way it once used to be. A great way to maintain a healthy level of independence is by nurturing your relationships and friendships away from your partner, as well as with them.

4.   Dropping Everything For Your Partner Immediately
There are times when it's perfectly acceptable to drop everything for your partner. If they're having an emergency, then absolutely go and help them – but don't abandon your life for anything less than this, except for rare occasions. If you're about to have a day of important meetings and your partner is feeling sad, wait till you're done with your obligations. Being sad is not an emergency. Your partner should be able to handle their emotions for a few hours. If you're planning on going to a friend's birthday party but your partner has a cold, do not cancel your original plans! When we get in the habit of abandoning our obligations for our partner, we send the message that nothing and no one else matters. This is a highly destructive attitude to take and one that will lead to a lot of regret in other areas of your life. Let professional and personal development be just as important as your partner.

5.   Expecting Your Partner to Always Cheer You Up
We can't avoid feelings of sadness, frustration, or even depression. During these low points, our relationship can be a great source of relief and happiness. If your partner does something special for you in your moment of sadness, this should be considered a bonus, not a necessity.

Unless your partner made a mistake which they're apologizing for, it should never be the responsibility of your loved one to make you feel better. It is reasonable to expect that they treat is with consideration, but our inner turmoil is our own to deal with and no one else's responsibility. A major sign of codependency is the expectation that our partner's will fix everything for us. It's essential that you learn the necessary tools to deal with your issues privately. Your partner has his or her own issues to deal with.

6. Saying You're "Fine" When You're Anything But

If you're trying to quit codependency, you need to learn how to talk to your partner honestly. Stop sweeping everything under the rug. This doesn't mean there needs to be a huge blowout or a big deal made about everything; it just means you need to be honest if something bothers you. When we dismiss our feelings, we risk allowing problematic behavior to continue. Furthermore, we raise the possibility of building resentment or dissatisfaction in the long-term. Both of these outcomes with affect your relationship negatively. For a healthy and happy relationship, learn to talk about your feelings in a constructive and open way. A good rule of thumb is to communicate in "I feel" statements as opposed to accusations, i.e. you would say "I feel upset about what you said" instead of "What you said was upsetting."

7. Frequent Interrogations

Every time we interrogate our partners, we demonstrate that we do not entirely trust them. If you have trust issues due to past trauma, there's a way to seek reassurance from your partner without resorting to interrogations. Instead of firing a hundred emotionally charged questions at your partner, try stating that you feel insecure and need them to reassure you. This is a more honest approach to the situation and it is a far more kind way to behave. When we interrogate our partners, this creates anxiety in them whether they did anything wrong or not. Let's not forget that interrogations are meant to intimidate – to extract an answer by forcing someone into submission. If you want to have a healthy dynamic with your partner, leave out all intimidation or scare tactics. This will only make your partner afraid of you and it could backfire on your relationship. Learn to build stronger trust or find kinder ways of getting the response you need.

8. Stalking Your Partner Online

It's no secret that trust is essential to building a strong relationship. For the same reason you shouldn't snoop through your partner's phone or interrogate them, you should also resist the urge to stalk them online. People who do this will frequently check their partner's social media page, keeping up with their latest 'likes,' comments, and shares. This modern-day habit of keeping tabs on our partner can easily get obsessive and lead to suspicions or upsets over nothing. Many codependents will engage in this behavior without even thinking of the deeper implications. Quit the habit of monitoring your partner's behavior. Talk out your issues with them or learn to let go.

9. Making Every Social Media Post About Your Partner

There are many signifiers of codependence that are unique to modern day and this is one of them. If nearly every post on your social media involves your partner then this is a big sign that your identity is highly dependent on them. As we've established, an identity that revolves around another person is a key symptom of codependency. In a healthy relationship, one's sense of self should be clearly defined outside of the relationship. Interests, hobbies, opinions, likes, and dislikes should not be dependent on the other person in the relationship. If you're looking for an easy codependent habit to quit, try this one. Explore your social media presence without it being so closely linked to your relationship.

10. Helping Your Partner with Everyday Adult Tasks

This screams 'codependency' like few other bad habits. It's completely normal to help your partner out every once in a while, especially if you have a little free time, but do not make it a habit unless they're doing something similar for you in return. If you have extra time to make your partner a packed lunch, then sure, why not? Have you made a routine of packing lunch while your partner makes dinner every night? That sounds like a great balance of tasks. But if you're doing this everyday and not getting anything back, then this is straight-up codependent behavior. In all that you do, ensure that you never 'baby' your partner. Do not perform tasks that all other adults are doing for themselves. If you can do it for yourself, your partner can do it for him or herself too. It's time to let your partner be the grown-up they are.

Believe or not, destructive and dysfunctional behavior are not just about abuse. They can also consist of small, everyday habits that appear harmless at first glance. Over time, however, they wear away at trust and the bond underneath a relationship. To make room for growth, start eliminating these harmful compulsions.

Chapter 6: Detachment Strategies

Underneath every codependency is an unhealthy level of attachment. Partners have merged their identities into one, to the point where they no longer feel they have a separate identity outside of their relationship. What's ironic is that attachment is usually formed through an attempt to create a unique identity. However, we only get ourselves further from this goal since this new identity is so interwoven with somebody else.

Not all codependent partnerships will have outright destructive tendencies but the severe attachment is no less harmful to the individuals involved. In order to break the codependency, both partners must learn to find a healthy detachment from each other. Healthy detachment still allows for expectations and dependency, but removes the sense of desperation and helplessness. Codependent people tend to find this idea intimidating because they feel like codependence is synonymous with love – but once they break this dynamic, they instantly feel liberated. Love that stems from want instead of need is far more fulfilling for everyone involved. To discover what this feels like, make use of these detachment strategies for a more empowering dynamic.

9 Great Habits that Start Healing Codependency

You know all about the bad habits that need to be broken – now, it's time to tell you about the great habits that should replace them. Implement these new practices into your daily life to start seeing a healthy detachment from your partner. By absorbing these new ways into your relationship dynamics, you'll immediately start feeling less codependent.

1. Respond, Don't React

Due to past trauma, some of us have certain reactions wired into our brain. Without even thinking about it, we can find ourselves giving into these impulses out of pure habit. For example, if you were cheated on in the past, you may find it triggering if your current partner has a close friend of the opposite sex. Whenever your partner mentions seeing them, you may immediately feel betrayed and angry, even when you have no reason to be. A good rule of thumb to avoid unnecessary upsets is to cut the impulse off before it takes control. Instead of simply reacting out of habit, take the time to really listen to what your partner is saying. Consider if what they're saying is actually unreasonable or if you're just overcome by bad memories. Respond to what your partner is telling you in the here and now, instead of something that happened in the past.

2. Nurture Your Wants & Needs

Don't lose yourself in your relationship. If there are any interests or hobbies calling out to you, why not pique your curiosity? Dive into new curiosities and continue exploring your established interests. Stop suppressing your wants, needs, curiosities, likes, and dislikes. Nurture and encourage everything that makes you *you*. This will strengthen your sense of self, ensuring your identity is still entirely yours even when you're in an intimate relationship. Having different needs and desires isn't just good for the sake of it; it allows both partners separate worlds to escape into so that they can always remember what makes them unique. This way, they never lose their life purpose and stay firmly connected to their essence.

3. Make Personal Space Non-Negotiable

Don't just *try* to get personal space sometimes; you need to make personal space a non-negotiable. Set aside a day or time when you get to have space to do whatever you want – and of course, without your partner. Stop seeing personal space as a daunting idea and start to recognize it as absolutely essential for maintaining your happiness in the long run. See it as a must-have. Even if you think you'll miss your partner, that's no reason to cling and never let go. Why wait till you're sick of them before you have personal space? Missing someone we get to be with later is an incredible joy. It means the love and excitement is still alive. By making personal space a core part of your lifestyle, you'll ensure that this love and excitement stays alive and doesn't fizzle out. Do whatever you enjoy and give each other space to breathe. This does wonders for every relationship.

4.   Be Accountable for Your Actions

As soon as you do this, you create an atmosphere of honesty, humility, and courage within the relationship. Being accountable for our actions and admitting when we've made a mistake can be difficult – but it shouldn't be. When we avoid accountability, we are essentially trying to say we are powerless and everything just happens to us – that it's not our fault because we have no influence over the situation. Why is this a good thing? When we're powerless we cannot take action to make things better. We become slaves to circumstance and the whims of other people. This is why being accountable is so transformative. You are recognizing your influence and control, and by doing so, you are also recognizing your capabilities of making things better. When one partner gets into the habit of taking accountability and owning up to their failures, the other partner (provided they are not a narcissist) begins to get comfortable doing the same. A couple that becomes accountable for their separate actions is a strong couple. There is significantly less upset and frustration in the relationship. Instead of needless blame and sour emotions, there can finally be a focus on solutions. The next time you make a mistake, tell your partner you realized what you did, that you're sorry, and you want to improve things next time. Do not play the blame game.

5. Call Out Your Partner for their Unhealthy Behavior

Just as you should be accountable for your actions, so should your partner. Sometimes it's not easy to recognize when we've made a mistake, especially when certain behaviors are routine. In this case, it's very important for the other partner to gently draw it to their attention. If they don't know, how can they improve themselves for the future? If you notice your partner displaying behavior that is unhealthy or even self-destructive, get into the habit of letting them know immediately. It's also essential that you do this constructively and with kindness. If you are angry and abusive, it is likely that they will respond negatively, adding further hindrances to the relationship's evolution. If your partner starts to guilt-trip you for wanting to spend time with your friends, address this codependent behavior. Say, "Honey, I felt like you were trying to guilt-trip me for seeing my friends and it worries me that we're resorting back to our codependent ways. How can we fix this for next time? I'd love it if we could find a solution so I can get some quality time with my friends. It's important to me that I see them sometimes." See, that's not so hard, is it?

6. Determine Your Personal and Professional Goals

Maintain a strong sense of self by continuing to grow and evolve. If you find yourself feeling stagnant or as though your relationship has consumed you, take time to sit down and reflect. Oftentimes we can lose direction because we haven't identified our wants and our goals. Think about what you'd like to accomplish in the near and distant future, then break these goals down into achievable steps. These can be professional goals, personal goals, or both. Is there a skill you'd like to take further? A new milestone you'd like to achieve? Would you like to lose or gain weight? Is there an artistic masterpiece you'd like to complete or at least get started on? There are numerous goals you can set for your life. Choose something that ignites excitement and joy in you. When we establish goals for ourselves, it becomes much easier to avoid codependency since we are instinctively trying to meet our own goals. It gives us something to strive for that is entirely about our own life and not directly connected to our partner. Make sure you always goals you're trying to meet, even if they are small goals.

7. Get an Outside Opinion

In the most extreme codependencies, both partners shy away from speaking to other people about their issues, especially those pertaining to their relationship. They have developed such an intense closeness to their partner that they feel they don't need anyone else. Unfortunately, this also means that when legitimate issues or problems arise in the relationship, they don't have anyone to tell. An outsider's perspective can be hugely beneficial, especially when it comes from a close friend or family member. Make sure neither you nor your partner shut out your respective support networks. They'll be able to tell when your codependency is getting too damaging. Learn to see this as helpful feedback and not just something inconvenient you'd rather not hear. When we're too close to a situation, it can be difficult to see everything as it is. Rely on your friends and family to tell you what you need to hear. Get in the habit of reaching out and maintaining your outside connections.

8. Say 'No' More Often

There's a huge misconception that if we love someone, we should let them do whatever they want. Hopefully by now, you've realized this could not be more wrong. Never saying 'no' to your partner is one of the key things that can lead to codependency. It essentially means you have no boundaries for your partner. When you get in the habit of saying 'no' to your partner, you're standing up for your needs and desires, conveying that they are just as important as your partner's. It is not cruel to say 'no' as oftentimes 'doormat' tendencies can lead to a quiet resentment in codependent partners. By setting boundaries, you're ensuring that you never exhaust yourself by giving more than you have. Down the road, this means you'll be happier, more fulfilled, and far more ready to be a good partner. The kindness you show your loved one will be born out of genuine love instead of necessity and obligation.

9. Solve Problems Together

When someone in a relationship makes a mistake, people tend to oversimplify the solution-finding process. They tend to think, "You made the mistake, so you should fix it. Figure it out and get back to me when things are better." We leave the person who made the mistake to come up with a solution on their own. Many couples believe this is the fair thing to do, but it's far from it. Healthy couples solve problems together. This does not mean both partners are at fault. It shows they recognize two heads are better than one. If you truly want to fix the situation and not just 'get even,' you should work alongside your partner to find a solution. Examine the problem at hand, what went wrong, and what could be better next time. Get in the habit of cooperating instead of making just one partner responsible for change.

4 Unique Challenges to Get Used to Healthy Detachment

If you're extremely codependent, the thought of detachment may sound scary to you. To simplify your next few steps, consider experimenting with the following challenges. These will help you get in the proper mindset for finding your own independence. At the end of each challenge, reunite with your partner and share your different experiences. See if you can have some fun with these challenges!

1. Draw Your Day

You don't need to have an artistic streak for this challenge – in fact, it might be more fun if you don't! For this challenge, both partners should separate for several hours and draw what they see, wherever they choose to go. They can take their pick of anything they see that day – it can be funny, serious, or even surrealist, if they so desire! Ideally, both partners shouldn't text each other except to discuss logistics about where and what time to meet up later. At the end of the day, both partners can reunite and show each other what they drew. If you're a terrible artist, laughing at your bad drawings could make for a hilarious evening. This challenge is one of the best since it allows people to get in touch with their creative side while also getting personal space. And the benefits don't end there! Partners always enjoy looking over each other's drawings and sharing the stories connected to what they saw.

2. Meet in the Middle

If there's an adventurous side to you, try the 'Meet in the Middle' challenge with your partner. Put simply: it requires both partners to explore two opposite or faraway locations and then meet up again halfway. This challenge can be scaled to suit your time frame and budget. If you're not able to travel internationally, there's no need to fret! Each partner can choose a city or town in the country that they've always wanted to explore. This works especially well if the other partner has already been there or doesn't care to go. Once both people have chosen their city or town, they can pinpoint a location that's roughly halfway. After traveling through and exploring separate locations, they can make their way to each other and meet in that halfway spot. If you have a bigger budget, consider doing this with countries. Solo travel is an empowering experience and couples, inevitably, find the 'halfway meetup' to be incredibly romantic.

3. The Gift Exchange

Just like 'Draw Your Day,' this challenge involves a couple separating for a few to several hours. There should be no communication whatsoever until it's time to reunite, later on in the day. The goal of their time apart should be to purchase, create, or just somehow procure a gift for their partner. The target can be one gift or more, depending on their respective budgets. It would also be wise for both partners to decide on a spending limit, so one person doesn't outspend the other. This is a great challenge to start off with since both partners can still feel close to each other in the pursuit of a gift for their loved one.

4. Outside-Inside

No excuses allowed for this one! One person is in charge of 'Outside' and the other is in charge of 'Inside.' For as long as it takes to finish, both partners must focus on their separate tasks without help from the other. Partners can only communicate over logistics or if they're asking for clarification. All other communication must be saved for after the challenge, when everything is complete. Here's a rundown of what each person is in charge of:

Outside - All errands that involve going out such as grocery shopping, sending mail, picking up tools or materials for repairs, refilling the car with gas, depositing a check or withdrawing money for rent, and many others. It can also include household chores if they take place outside, e.g. gardening, yard work, shed repairs, etc.

Inside - All duties regarding the inside of the home and general housekeeping. This includes doing laundry, making beds, cleaning and dusting the home, tidying and reorganizing clutter, doing dishes, and all other home-related chores.

Whoever finishes first gets to have free time to do whatever they want! The only condition? They must stay away from their partner until all chores are completed.

Why not create your own challenge? For the best outcome, both partners should be separated for as long as possible while focusing on a clearly defined goal or enjoying a distraction.

Chapter 7: Personal Space & Self-Care

We've spoken a lot about personal space and self-care, but some of you may be wondering, "What exactly does that entail?" or "What do I do once I have personal space?" If you're at the extreme end of codependent, you may need some ideas for your next self-care sesh. As we've established, this is crucial for maintaining a healthy level of independence in your relationship. When partners continue to practice this in a relationship, they become stronger, more courageous individuals that see more life fulfillment in the long run. If you're intimidated by the thought of having temporary separation, understand that it's only difficult for one reason: you're breaking a fixed routine! It's in no way indicative of the effects it will ultimately have. Destructive or not, patterns are difficult to break – but once you succeed, your life blossoms in ways you could never have imagined.

6 Reasons Why Personal Space Heals Couples

Before you can come up with excuses for skipping the rest of this chapter, let's examine the benefits of personal space. On the days you're overwhelmed by anxiety, when you just want to cling and never let go, turn back to this section. This is why personal space is vital for healing codependency:

1. It Makes You a Stronger Person

When we are given space to do our own thing, we use coping and self-management tools that we stop using in the presence of our close loved ones. If we have a need, we learn to take care of it on our own. We learn to provide our own entertainment. And we can finally listen and assess our own thoughts, without influence from an outside party. That pang you feel when you're by yourself and you really wish someone was there with you – that's your mind refusing to use your own self-management tools. When we have someone around us, we don't have to use them as much. They can help us perform tasks, entertain us, and they provide us with as many distractions as we desire. This feels good in the same way sitting on the couch, instead of going to work, feels good. It allows us to not do any work, but it damages our ability to fend for ourselves and be self-sufficient. If you don't learn to be strong now, it'll be a hundred times more difficult in the future. Personal space gives us the opportunity to self-manage again and this brings a lot of benefits with it.

2.   Reconnecting to Our Individuality Makes Us Happier

When we get personal space, we our reminded of what makes us different. Instead of merging with our partner's identity, we remember our own and what exactly makes us unique. When we reconnect with this part of ourselves, we instantly feel happier. Why? It's simple. We all want to feel special. No one wants to feel like they've become exactly like something else. Those who do are under the mistaken impression that merging identities is the cure to not feeling special. This, of course, could not be further from the truth. To truly feel one-of-a-kind and unique, we need to connect to something deep in ourselves. This part of us can only be accessed through sufficient time alone. As much as you love your partner, too much time together can make you forget what makes you different.

3.   There's More to Talk About Later On

If you're always with each other, you're receiving the same general experience at the same time. This can be special too, of course; you can discuss events as they unfold around you and enjoy sharing in the same experience. But don't forget, there's also enjoyment to be had in having different experiences and telling the story later on. Two partners that reunite after a long day apart can relay the stories and events of the day to one another, relishing the storytelling and the surprise element that comes with it. When we're always with our partner, we miss out on the fun of catching up.

4. You Can Get Sick of Great Things, Too – Don't Let This Happen!

You may love and cherish your partner deeply. You may even think your relationship is the best thing in the world and you're so meant for each other that nothing can ruin what you have. I hate to break it to you: too much time together can, indeed, ruin it. Let's say you discovered the world's best pancakes. You found them so delicious you decided to have them for every meal. At first, having your favorite food three times a day seemed like heaven – but what about after a few months? Or a few years? You'd definitely start to get sick of it. Eventually, you'd start to crave literally *anything* else. It doesn't matter how objectively good those pancakes are or how much you enjoyed them in the beginning. If you overdo it, you won't want anything more to do with them. The same goes for you and your partner. Without personal space, the relationship starts to feel suffocating. This will inevitably lead to a more strained partnership.

5. It Reminds You of Why You're Together

When we are constantly with someone or something that we love, we start to take them for granted. We get so accustomed to quick and easy access that we forget how special it is to have access at all. Couples that make personal space a part of their lifestyle experience a lot more gratitude towards their partner. When they're together, they're reminded of the joy that their significant other brings to their life. The periods of being apart create a contrast against the times they are together. This immediately highlights the positive differences their

75

relationship makes. In turn, this makes every moment together seem more special. Partners will appreciate each other much more and be happier in the long run.

6.   Happier People Create More Lasting Relationships
Codependence is formed when couples are too anxious or insecure to let each other go. Ironically, learning to do so can actually make the chances of staying together (happily) more likely. Consider everything we've covered so far. There will be more excitement, you won't get sick of each other, *you'll* be happier and so will your partner. Two happy, strong individuals make a happy, strong couple. To ensure lasting satisfaction, there needs to be room to grow. By giving each other space, you're allowing each other space to evolve into better selves. Couples that do this thrive better than the rest.

10 Ways to Accelerate Self-Growth While You Have Personal Space

Codependent people struggle to fill their time when they finally have personal space. Many begin to feel anxiety, not sure what to do with themselves now that their partner isn't there. It's helpful to note this only happens because it is a break from their usual routine. It can be overcome with practice. Personal space is a great time to finally focus on self-growth and make strides towards accomplishing your personal goals. Making the effort to always keep your goals in sight will help you ward off your codependent leanings. Consider the many ways you can do this:

1.   Learn a New Skill
Is there a talent you secretly wish you had? When was the last time you thought 'I wish I could do that'? A workshop or class is a fantastic thing to add to a schedule and it's a great use of personal time. It can

be anything from painting and photography classes to kung fu lessons. The sky's the limit when it comes to learning. You could even choose to improve a skill that leads to a higher income down the road. Perfecting a new skill will remind you of your worth and capabilities beyond your relationship. Have fun with this one. The world is your oyster!

2. Go to the Gym

Make gym sessions part of your weekly routine and you'll see benefits beyond just your appearance. Not only will you look fitter and more toned, but most importantly, you'll *feel* stronger. And you'll instantly see a boost in your level of self-esteem and confidence. Working out is a great way to prove to yourself that you can overcome adversity – this determination and strength will extend beyond your time at the gym, improving your relationship and likely even your professional confidence. Take care of your body and your entire mindset will reflect this positive transformation.

3. See a Therapist

It's time to remove the stigma around therapy! You don't need a mental health condition in order to see a therapist. Having a session once a week or every couple of weeks is a great way to destress and declutter the mind. Getting restless emotions and thoughts out of the way gives you more time to focus on what really matters. Therapy can be especially beneficial for people in a codependent relationship. A neutral figure will be able to point out when codependent habits are surfacing and help you evolve out of them. They can help you tackle the root cause of your issues so you never again have to call yourself 'codependent.'

4. Experiment with Cooking Healthier Meals

We all know how to cook *something* in the kitchen, but how many delicious, truly healthy meals can you cook? In your spare time, why not experiment in the kitchen with some body-nourishing foods. When we focus our attention on feeding ourselves, our minds find a calm center. Why? Because we are going back to basics and doing something that literally keeps us alive. We are giving attention to the fundamentals of our being and this can be meditative. Try and cook with new ingredients, have fun with new flavors, and see what delicious creations you can come up with.

5. Plan Your Future and Set Goals

Now that you have some alone time, why not see if you can define your goals for the near and distant future? What would you like to accomplish? Where would you like to go? What are some habits you'd like to break and some better habits you'd like to pick up? While you're doing this, try and make your first draft of goals without considering what your partner (or anyone else) would say about them. Just focus on your goals and dreams. Once you clearly identify what these are, weight out how important each one is to you. How happy will you be if you achieve each one? Will the inability to achieve a certain goal lead to unhappiness? Answer these questions before thinking of what your partner would say. Consider making the goals that would make you deeply happy a non-negotiable.

6. Read a Good Book

They say the world's most successful entrepreneurs read dozens of books a year. It's no wonder why. Not only is reading entertaining, but it can broaden your horizons in ways that change your perspective and outlook for the better. Whether it's fiction or nonfiction, reading brings many benefits including memory improvement and stress reduction. Over time, you'll find your vocabulary expanding and it may even enhance your writing skills. Incorporate more reading time into your schedule (now that you have more peace and quiet!) and you'll supercharge that mind of yours in no time.

7. Start a Creative Project

You don't need to be an artistic genius to start a creative project. It's as simple as choosing a medium you enjoy and having fun with it. Encouraging your own creativity helps you destress and in the long run, improves your problem-solving abilities. Studies have even shown that creativity enhances one's ability to adapt to new changes. The next time you have time to yourself, why not try painting or sketching? Or pick up an instrument and learn to sing?

8. Learn to Develop a Growth Mindset

As you pursue new hobbies and skills in your spare time, try and develop a growth mindset. A fixed mindset is driven by the belief that everyone is born with certain talents and gifts, and all those who are not 'gifted' will never achieve the same level of brilliance. The growth mindset comes as a firm opposition to this, asserting that we can indeed reach the same level of brilliance if we persist and continue improving ourselves. While you have personal space, try to absorb this growth mindset into your mental space. Not only will this help you improve certain skills, it will also help you grow out of your codependency. You don't have to be codependent forever; a growth mindset will ensure you leave your old habits behind for good.

9. Take Breaks from Tech

While you're taking a break from your partner, why not take a Break with a capital B from all the chaos of the modern world? You can choose whatever timeframe you're most comfortable with – but it should pose a little bit of a challenge! For at least a couple of hours, turn off all your communication and entertainment devices. Completely disconnect from all digital distractions and do not communicate with your partner in any way during this time. Feel free to do whatever you like during this time as long as you are in charge of creating your own entertainment (do not go to a bar and watch their TV!) and you're allowing yourself to be alone with your thoughts. Practicing No Tech time can decrease anxiety over time as you begin to get used to silence and temporary disconnection.

10. Have a Conversation with a Stranger

This may seem like an odd suggestion, but learning to be comfortable around strangers has a number of different benefits. Not only do you improve your social skills, but you learn to become adaptable to different situations and different personalities. You also have no idea who you might meet! There are connections just waiting to be made all around you. Expanding your circle of friends is a great way to ensure you don't rely too heavily on your partner.

12 Self-Care Ideas to Make You Feel Like a Million Bucks

Of course, personal space should also be about self-care. When codependents are completely wrapped up in each other, they forget to take care of their own self. Often we don't realize how much we need self-care until we finally experience it. The result: we're calm, centered, and at peace in every single way. This puts is in a better mood, making us more pleasant individuals. In turn, this makes us better partners.

There's no need to reserve self-care for when we're completely alone. Self-care should be part of your routine and you can do it by yourself or with your partner close by. That's up to you. However you choose to care for yourself, make sure you always make time for it so it can be a consistent part of your life.

1. Bubble Baths

You've probably seen it happen in movies. During times of relaxation, a character is neck deep in a bubble bath surrounded by candles. Why not try it in real life? Bubbles or no bubbles, candles or bathroom lights, music or silence: the choice is yours. Discover what kind of environment helps you achieve a deep calm and try to get to that quiet place in your mind. Forget the world for a moment and relax.

2. Massage

Getting a massage requires no effort from you. Just find a spa or masseuse that you like the sound of, and enjoy being pampered. A massage session makes brilliant self-care because the kneading opens up the body and – of course – it just *feels* amazing. The gentle pressure all over the body relieves stress by releasing dopamine, reducing anxiety and instantly making you feel more calm, no matter what. It doesn't need to be complicated; just lay down and allow yourself to feel good.

3. Coffee and a Good Book

Since the dawn of hipster cafes, the coffee-and-a-book routine has become a brilliant modern way of achieving self-care. Get out of your space and spend a few hours in a coffee shop. Order a steaming cup of coffee or a creamy hot chocolate, find your spot, and finally delve into that great book you've heard so much about. Believe it or not, just getting out of your personal space can reduce anxiety. The coffee-and-a-book routine allows you to simplify your life for just a moment. All you have to do is enjoy your comfy spot, focus on your book, whilst nourishing your belly with warm, rich goodness.

4. Go Shopping

Let's preface this by saying: don't go overboard! Know what your budget and stick to it. And other than that? Have fun and treat yourself to whatever makes you feel good. There's a reason the term 'retail therapy' exists. When we shop, we get to indulge our wants and needs. This is good practice for the codependent who tends to be focused on other people's wants and needs. Take this moment to shut your codependent brain out and consider what purchase would excite you in the here and now.

5. Get a Makeover

Sometimes there's no better way to feel good than by making yourself *look* good. There are no rules to getting a makeover – just have fun experimenting with your appearance with the goal of making yourself feel attractive. If you're female, consider purchasing the services of a makeup artist. Both genders can enjoy getting a few different outfits for their wardrobe or freshening up with a new haircut. The possibilities are endless!

6. Talk to Friends

Talking and laughing with friends is its own form of therapy. While you're engaging in self-care, why not have a catch up session with some of your most trusted friends? Not only does this provide stress relief but it's been proven that spending time with friends leads to a longer lifetime and improved mental health. Whether you decide to indulge at a great restaurant or have a fun night in watching Netflix or a game, make sure that time with friends is a regular session in your schedule.

7. Write in a Journal

Journaling is great for codependent couples because it allows you to get in touch with your feelings. To keep the peace, codependents are known to shut their thoughts and feelings out – something that does not bode well for the health of the relationship. Journaling can help you declutter your mind and destress, allowing you to organize your thoughts and observe your inner world. Many people choose to write in their journals in the early morning or right before bedtime, as a way of calming the mind for the day or for restful sleep.

8. Meditate

When looking for the best self-care methods, meditation is suggested so often that it tends to elicit a roll of the eyes. There's a good reason why meditation is raved about; it has real, lasting benefits that genuinely make a difference to your mental well-being and life. To meditate successfully, one must try to clear their mind of all thoughts and simply be in the moment. To get started, try and focus your breath, and nothing else. Ideally, this should be done in a quiet space where one can sit down without being disturbed. Make meditation part of your self-care routine and you'll soon see reduced stress and anxiety, and an enhanced self-awareness and attention span.

9. Go For a Drive or Walk

This self-care method requires nothing but energy and time. Choose any starting point at all and just take a walk or drive from there onwards with no destination in sight. Just explore and keep going forwards. The purpose of this drive is to clear your mind and to have time alone with yourself, while still experiencing the motion of moving forwards. Going for a walk or drive is known to be emotionally healing; it allows you to be in full control of your path and destination, just going wherever you please and letting your thoughts find peace.

10. Redecorate

A fun way to achieve self-care is by redecorating your space. This could be anywhere you like. It could be your desk at work, your bedroom, or even your entire house. Redecorating can be incredibly fun as it allows us to use the creative side of our brain – but more than this, it is also an act of reclaiming our space and practicing our control over our surroundings. Make aesthetically pleasing choices and see if you can rearrange your belongings for the most convenience possible. Organize and decorate your space so that it becomes your own personal sanctuary. By the end, you should feel comfortable, relaxed, and inspired in your newly decorated space.

11. Exercise

Exercise isn't just a way to see more self-growth, it's also a great way to engage in self-care. It's only important that you don't overdo it and exhaust yourself. Whether it's a leisurely walk through the park or an intense session of pilates, exercise ensures that your body stays strong and capable. Many people think that exercise is so hard it can't possibly be self-care, but this is just a sign that you need it more than ever. Exercising allows us to reconnect with our vessel and to be more in tune with its needs and abilities. The rush of endorphins also means you'll instantly feel more positive about yourself and life in general.

12. Practice Gratitude

Believe it or not, it's been proven that practicing gratitude makes a person more happy. By training the brain to notice and be thankful for the positive things in life, we instantly begin to operate from a mindset of abundance. This improves our sense of self-esteem, our ability to empathize, and it even improves our quality of sleep. To begin practicing gratitude, find a place where you can begin making notes about what you're grateful for. This can be a special gratitude journal or it can be on the Notes app on your phone. Every day list down three things that you're grateful for in your life. Try and be as specific as possible. Remember that these don't have to be grand parts of your life, it can be as simple as the fantastic lunch you had or a great workout session. Just make sure whatever it is, you feel genuinely grateful for it.

Do not feel daunted by the idea of personal space. It's a chance for you to recalibrate, reenergize, and do what you need to do to sustain your own inner strength. It's a time to reconnect with the activities you enjoy and the purpose of your life. Learn not to see it as separation from your partner, but instead as powerful fuel for a healthy relationship.

Chapter 8: Healing Codependency For Good

We've broken down personalities of codependent partners, highlighted the habits that need to be eradicated, as well as the habits you need to start bringing into your life – but that's not all you need moving forward. The urges that lead to codependency run deep. Underneath the little habits and practices are some key and highly essential lessons. The smaller practices will certainly help in building a healthier day-to-day dynamic, but without absorbing these core lessons, you may find yourself relapsing back to square one. During particularly trying periods, feel free to return back to this chapter to remind yourself of what's important.

The Lessons that Break Codependency

- 'Tough Love' is Necessary – Embrace It

Don't shy away from the notion of tough love. Simply put, tough love is when we give our loved ones certain boundaries or constraints with the intention of helping them grow in the long run. Even if they don't realize it, tough love is for *their* benefit. To heal codependency for good, you need to start embracing practices of tough love. This means saying no and setting limits even when you feel sorry for them and want to say yes. Codependents may struggle with guilt at first so it's important that you make a mindset shift during these moments. Instead of focusing on their reaction in the current moment, think of the benefits they'll see down the road. Think of the life-altering lessons this will teach them and how life will reward them for it if they persist. Do not be swayed by the temporary discomfort and focus all your attention on the potential growth of the situation. Tough love is a different kind of loving behavior, but it is loving no less.

- Needs are Tools, not Enemies

In codependent relationships, the enabler tends to see their needs as obstacles. After all, how can they take care of their partners needs when their own are getting in the way? For enablers to continue breaking their codependent patterns, they need to stop seeing their needs as inconveniences. Our wants and needs are tools. They tell us about our state of mind and what we need in our life to find satisfaction. Our needs give us the direction we desire. It tells us what we need for growth and what you need to sustain yourself emotionally and psychologically. Needs are, indeed, tools and indicators of growth. Do not shun them away or the urges will only become stronger. We become unhappy when we ignore these urges and try to suppress them. A need signifies a lack and if left unchecked, this can lead to a kind of emotional or mental depletion. Your needs are akin to the red light that goes on when your car starts to need more gas. These lights do you a favor by letting you know when they need something to keep going as normal. Treat your needs the same way. Do not let those red lights start flashing!

- Nothing Changes if You Don't Change

By now you've probably been faced with some harsh truths about your behavior and relationship. It's profoundly important that you don't stop here. The knowledge that you need to change is not enough in itself to create change. You feel unsatisfied, unfulfilled, like your relationship could be much better, and you're right – now do something about it. Use feelings of dissatisfaction as fuel to start taking action. Your codependency will not heal if you don't begin working with your partner to find a healthier dynamic. If you find yourself reverting back to your old ways, expect to revert back to your old feelings of frustration. If you want better for your relationship, *be* better.

- Clinginess and Obsession are Not the Same as Love

When you're completely wrapped up in your partner, it can be easy to think this obsession is equivalent to love. There's a big misconception that giving until you have nothing left and merging your identity with your partner is what true love means, but this only results in codependency. Moving forward, try to shift your perspective on what love means. Remember that love isn't just about how you are as a single unit, it's also about how the relationship affects you as an individual. Does the relationship empower you to achieve your own dreams and goals? Or does it make you feel like giving up on the rest of your life? Does the relationship remind you of who you really are? Or does it completely eradicate your unique identity? Think of love in terms of the long-term future that you're building with your partner, not just about how instantly gratifying is. Try and understand that love doesn't take over our life; it helps the rest of our life to blossom. The more you cling to your partner, the less time and space there is for the rest of your life. Real love is about two whole people who come together in their full power, not two halves trying desperately to make a whole.

- Stop Feeling Defeated by Rejection

There's a reason why both partners fuel this cycle of codependency; they're afraid of what would happen if they stopped. The enabler is worried, on some level, about not being useful and the enabled partner is worried about being forgotten. Although both partners have different ways of coping, they're both trying to ensure they remain loved by the other partner. Why? Because the thought of losing their codependent partner is far too painful. Unfortunately, this type of mentality can backfire. When we are driven to act a certain way out of deep insecurity around loss and rejection, it can become a self-fulfilling prophecy. As difficult as it seems, both partners need to learn to be okay with the possibility of not being in their codependent relationship. In other words, they need to get comfortable with the idea of being single. When they think of losing their partner, it's normal to feel deep sadness but they shouldn't feel like their world will end. Getting comfortable with the idea doesn't mean you want it to happen – it simply means that if it's right, you'll accept it. At the end of the day, rejection lets us know what's right for us and what isn't. Instead of trying to avoid rejection from your partner at all costs, learn to see it as a way to measure your compatibility. If you're rejected after trying your best, then it wasn't meant for you. One day you'll discover what *is* meant for you and you'll be fine.

What to Do If…?

You're trying to break a codependency and that's a big deal. Many scenarios will arise that leave you feeling confused and unsure of what the 'right' thing to do is for the health of your relationship. The next time you find yourself 'stuck,' turn back to this page. When you find yourself faced with any of these scenarios, this is what you should do:

- Your partner is not listening to your boundaries

By the time you finish this book, you'll likely feel motivated to strive for a healthier relationship. Unfortunately, you can't control how your partner feels. It's possible he or she isn't quite ready to make new changes. One of the ways they'll make this known is by refusing to abide by your newly set boundaries. If you make an agreement to split up chores, you may find that your partner still doesn't do their fair share, leaving you with most of the work.

Before you determine the best way to respond, answer these questions: how many times have you had to remind your partner of the boundaries? How many strikes have there been? How disrespected do you feel? Your intuition is a strong way to measure this situation. If you feel like your partner is trying their best but they're just struggling to let go of old habits, then be firm with them. Don't shy away from showing them you're angry or upset. Make it clear that this means a lot to you. If you feel disrespected and like your partner genuinely isn't trying, then reconsider your involvement in this relationship. You're trying your best and it's only fair your partner tries too. You're ready for a better relationship and as long as your partner is stuck in their old ways, they'll hold you back from growth too. You deserve better.

- Your partner is exaggerating their ailments as a way of rebelling against your new boundaries

You've tried to set boundaries with your partner and they've responded by exaggerating their condition. They are doing everything they can to make sure they appear more helpless. Hopefully, you know why by now. They want to keep the cycle going. They are likely afraid and nervous about the new turn your relationship is taking and they want you to start behaving like your old self.

Remember that your partner has been taught to equate enabling with love. This change of behavior is probably making them feel insecure, wondering how they'll continue getting love from you if you no longer feel the need to help them. Try and point out this behavior, gently. Draw what they are doing to their attention and explain why they are behaving this way. They may not even realize it and may be reacting purely out of insecurity. After this, continue to be firm with your boundaries but make an extra effort to show them love in ways that do not encourage codependence. If they enjoy receiving gifts, give them flowers or anything that encourages a new hobby – but all the while, do not back down on making them do their chores. Replace codependent behavior with other loving behavior.

- Your partner is suspicious of you whenever you have personal space

Since you and your partner are so used to spending a lot of time together, it can be jarring once you finally add personal space to your daily lives. As a way to cope, your partner may even become suspicious, believing that your behavior is caused by a more malicious ulterior motive. After all, they're used to seeing love as synonymous with time together. It will take time to adjust to this new perspective and it may result in resistance. They may even fire off a few accusations. For example, they may believe that the real reason you want space is to make time for cheating or because you're trying to break up with them in a kind way. These are some of the many accusations that enablers may hear.

See this behavior for what it is. Your partner has been taught that love means clinging to each other so naturally they think the reverse means you don't care about them. Obviously this isn't true, so take the time to gently reassure them. Remind them that the reason you're trying to change is because you want to ensure your relationship succeeds. Personal space is a way to make sure your relationship is healthy and secure, not desperate and clingy. Come up with ways you can reassure your partner without resorting to codependent behavior. Similar to the previous scenario, show them love in new ways, such as buying them a gift every now and then or writing them a heartfelt card.

- Your partner still can't take care of him or herself, even though you've given them space

As we've established, overhelping takes away autonomy and empowerment. To help your partner reconnect with their inner strength, you've likely given them space to learn how to take care of

91

their own needs. This is a positive move, on your part. However, you may find that your partner is still unable to help themselves. They're trying but they're failing. They're incompetent, getting things wrong all the time, and overall, not doing as good of a job as you used to do. In these moments, it'll be tempting to revert back to your old behavior. Watching them fail will make you want to help them again. If they're truly struggling, it's alright to give them a little bit of assistance, but other than this, try to stay firm. Otherwise, you may find yourself regressing. They're struggling because this is new to them. You've had your whole life to learn how to do it the right way, but they're only learning now. It will take some time. Expect it to take some time. Be gentle with them and do what you can to support them as they learn, but do not do the work for them. If your partner has trouble making their own food, buy them a new cookbook or pay for a cooking lesson or two – but do not give in and start making all their lunches for them again! Have patience and do what you can to foster growth.

- You've started to feel utterly useless and worthless

Until now, you've gotten by as the 'fixer' in your relationship. You got accustomed to helping your partner with every little thing and easing their pain whenever you could. But let's not forget, it's not just about what your partner receives from you; your satisfaction comes in the form of feeling needed. When you know you're helping your partner, you feel useful. You feel like you're doing something that matters. Breaking out of codependent habits means you're trying not to overhelp and this new change has caused you to feel a little useless. This may even result in some depression.

Remind yourself that you *are* helping by stepping back. By doing this, you're allowing your partner to learn their lessons and achieve self-growth. Understand that when you're not in a codependent relationship, helping and being useful manifests in different behavior. You're accustomed to the codependent way of 'helping' – which is actually enabling. When we *really* help someone, we do what's best for them. And in this case, *not* overhelping is what's best for your partner. Recognize that what you're really craving is the instant gratification that comes from enabling your partner. By not forcing them to do anything, you're allowing them to do what pleases them in the moment. This may look like it's good for them, but in reality, it is the furthest thing from helping. Remember this distinction and resist the urge to overhelp at all costs.

This journey won't always be easy. In fact, at times you'll struggle and feel like it's too difficult to handle. Of course it's hard – after all, you're breaking response patterns that have been hardwired into your brain. What's important is that you recognize the hardship for what it is. It's growth. Keep these core lessons at the center of all your decisions and you'll soon be able to proudly say, "No, I'm not codependent."

Conclusion

Congratulations on completing *No More Codependency*! By making it to this page, you've taken great strides towards a more sustainable and healthy relationship dynamic. This is wonderful news – not just for you, but also for your partner. You've proven that you are truly committed to a happier future with your significant other and that you're willing to do what it takes to quit your codependent ways. You are so much closer to success than you think! If you need more motivation, all you have to do is turn back to this book. Everything you need is right here.

Hopefully, this book has empowered you to keep making these big, powerful strides. It's important you remember that codependent relationships are not a life sentence; relationship coaches and psychologists everywhere agree that codependencies can, indeed, be healed with time. By adhering to the helpful rules and tips in this book, you'll soon see your relationship in a whole new light. You'll be a happier, more fulfilled individual and your relationship will blossom in turn. What's important is that you continue to persist and remain self-aware.

We've covered the in-depth details of codependency, identifying what it really means and what exactly makes it different to everyday dependence on our loved ones. It's important that you recognize this distinction as there's no need to eliminate all of your dependent behavior – some of it is perfectly normal. By now, you're well aware of the difference between the two. Codependent behavior doesn't mean never depending on our partner. It simply means having a healthy level of dependence and knowing who you are without your partner.

94

Before you move forward, it's essential that you figure out which codependent partner you are. Are you the enabler or the enabled? Try to approach this question without any denial. We've covered the likely backgrounds of each partner and it's possible you saw yourself in those descriptions. Perhaps you were even able to pinpoint the exact relationship in your childhood that gave you this codependent mindset. Now that you've finished this book, try and work through those memories. Which early relationship taught you to be codependent? Delve deeply into yourself and recognize that this early relationship was likely very dysfunctional. Treating your relationship the same way will only result in the same dysfunctions. You don't want that, do you? Of course not.

Once you commit to change, you'll need to start laying down some boundaries. This means saying 'no' and setting some rules where necessary. It means conveying to your partner, in some way, that you'll no longer be fixing every little thing that goes wrong. Doing this can be difficult, especially since you're not used to it. You may even have feelings of guilt or uncertainty around how to enforce them. Pay close attention to the tips we've covered and you'll soon see boundaries as completely natural. You'll suddenly find yourself with far more energy, now that you're no longer exhausted from over-exerting and doing more than your fair share.

Aside from this, it's also important that you and your partner work on building your sense of self. This may mean developing stronger self-esteem and self-awareness. Using the affirmations and exercises in this book, you can begin rewiring your psyche to produce more positive thoughts about yourself. How can you make the most of your gifts and positive qualities if you never realize they exist? Whether you realize it or not, self-esteem is a big part of healing codependency. You need to recognize that you are enough and that you are wonderful, even without a partner at your side. By creating a more positive inner dialogue, you'll help your relationship thrive.

After learning about boundaries and developing self-esteem, you were faced with some big challenges. Namely, destructive behavior. Hopefully, you were motivated and inspired to finally eliminate these harmful habits from your life. You can't evolve if you don't get rid of the obstacles. Once you've identified what these obstacles are, you can work hard on moving past them. Now that you understand the cycle of narcissistic abuse, you can hopefully recover from any abuse you've endured. If you're staying in a relationship with a narcissist, hold on tight. It may be a turbulent ride. Turn back to the section on narcissistic abuse and do your best to enact the changes that were listed – otherwise, you may find yourself stuck in a cycle that never ends. Remember this: if you don't change, nothing will!

With new detachment strategies and exercises under your belt, you can finally discover independence. Allow this to feel liberating because it is. Have fun with the challenges and enjoy how it feels to finally have personal space. By now, you'll know all about the importance of personal time and space. The next time you find yourself lost about what to do with yourself, rest assured you've got a solid list of ideas for what to do. Consider engaging in an activity that promotes self-growth or refreshes you through self-care. You need both in equal measure!

The core lessons that are integral to healing codependency have been summed up into bite-sized pieces. Turn back to the final chapter, if you ever find yourself wavering. Remind yourself of these lessons and make sure that every change you make is fueled by them. If a difficult scenario arises with your partner, this chapter will also give you ideas for what to do. There's always a solution as long as both partners are committed to growth. Don't let 'enabler' and 'enabled' define your life together. Explore your individuality, learn healthy detachment, and shower your entire life (not just your relationship) in love. Show yourself the same affection you're capable of giving someone else, and you'll move mountains.

CPSIA information can be obtained
at www.ICGtesting.com
Printed in the USA
LVHW051637180122
708825LV00005B/673

9 781648 660610